There are those who write books because they have an idea. Real Talk Kim wrote this one because she has a mandate. Her heart is to help you move beyond your "stuck" situation, and she's uniquely qualified as a result of the painful personal experiences she lived through herself. And she's not afraid to show you her scars.

As her pastor during a tumultuous time in her life, I have seen the transformation from an insecure young woman to a powerfully anointed woman of God. With keen insight and endearing humor, Kim speaks with authority and the redemptive love of God in her newest book, *When Your Bad Meets His Good*.

As her spiritual father, I'm so proud of her and this dynamic message that's touching the hearts of an entire generation. With so much fake news all around us, Kim's book is like a breath of fresh air. *When Your Bad Meets His Good* is transparent, timely, and transformative.

—Dr. Rod Parsley
Pastor and Founder, World Harvest Church

One thing that I absolutely love about Kim Jones-Pothier is that her nickname, Real Talk Kim, suits her perfectly! Her refreshing honesty about her past pain and her refusal to play the blame game make her an authentic voice, especially in the realm of relationships. If we could finally overcome self, we'd see all the incredible good that God wants to do in us and through us! Kim gets it exactly right! *If you have a heartbeat, you have a purpose!*

—Nicole Crank
Senior Pastor, FaithChurch.com

In *When Your Bad Meets His Good*, Kim Jones-Pothier—Real Talk Kim—equips us with a biblically sound revelation that will enable us to shake off the past and grab ahold of everything that God has predestined for us.

Pastor Kim is without a doubt one of the most anointed and gifted voices on the planet today. This book will not only touch you; it will transform you!

—Samuel Rodriguez
President, National Hispanic Christian Leadership Conference (NHCLC)
Lead Pastor, New Season

We don't know if there's a more in-your-face, unapologetically bold, and dynamic woman of God on social media today. Pastor Kimberly Jones-Pothier, @RealTalkKim, has taken ministry and now Instagram by storm with her messages and impactful posts. God has used her energy and enthusiasm for sharing the unadulterated truth to spread the beautiful message of grace and the gospel and touch the lives of millions all over the world. We love Pastor Kim and firmly believe that any book she's put her energy into will be a must-read. We will be the first to purchase!

—Tyrese and Samantha Gibson

In Kim's new book, *When Your Bad Meets His Good*, my friend keeps it real, relevant, and revelatory! This is a practical book of inspiration and instruction to show a person how to turn pain into power! She's done it and can show you how. Get the book, and let the transformation begin!

—Bishop Dale C. Bronner, DMin
Founder and Senior Pastor, Word of Faith Family Worship Cathedral

WHEN YOUR BAD MEETS
HIS GOOD

FIND PURPOSE IN YOUR PAIN

WHEN YOUR BAD MEETS
HIS GOOD

FIND PURPOSE IN **YOUR PAIN**

KIMBERLY JONES-POTHIER

CHARISMA
HOUSE

Most CHARISMA HOUSE BOOK GROUP products are available at special quantity discounts for bulk purchase for sales promotions, premiums, fund-raising, and educational needs. For details, write Charisma House Book Group, 600 Rinehart Road, Lake Mary, Florida 32746, or telephone (407) 333-0600.

WHEN YOUR BAD MEETS HIS GOOD by Kimberly Jones-Pothier
Published by Charisma House
Charisma Media/Charisma House Book Group
600 Rinehart Road
Lake Mary, Florida 32746
www.charismahouse.com

Visit the author's website at https://RealTalkKim.com or www .whenyourbadmeetshisgood.com.

Library of Congress Cataloging-in-Publication Data:
An application to register this book for cataloging has been submitted
to the Library of Congress.
International Standard Book Number: 978-1-62999-545-8
E-book ISBN: 978-1-62999-546-5

While the author has made every effort to provide accurate internet
addresses at the time of publication, neither the publisher nor the
author assumes any responsibility for errors or for changes that occur
after publication.

18 19 20 21 22 — 987654321
Printed in the United States of America

Where do I even begin to give the proper love and honor to my beautiful mom? Mom, you mean the entire world to me. I never dreamed that one day we would be working together writing best sellers. God knew. He directed your path as you retired from pastoring and became available to assist me. Who would have imagined that you would use the writing skills you used at a young age in the newspaper field to assist me in flowing so beautifully?

This is the third book we have written together, and God knew that having a mom-and-daughter team was just what was needed to paint the most beautiful pictures to help millions get free.

I love you to the moon and back a million times, and I am so honored that God gave me the blessing of getting to call you my mom and very best friend. Thank you for being so selfless, devoted, and committed to your family. You are our angel on earth. There is nobody like you, Elizabeth Ann Jones. Thank you! I love you!

CONTENTS

ACKNOWLEDGMENTS

I'D LIKE TO say thank you to my family, which is the greatest support system in the world. Morgan and Lyncoln, my most amazing gifts from God, I could never have asked for any sons greater than you two. You are my why and my heartbeat. I will spend the rest of my life letting you know in so many ways how much I appreciate your hanging in there with me through my journey. You are two amazing young men!

Mark, you have truly been my gift from God, and I could not be traveling the world and pouring into thousands if you were not my wind in my sails. You allow me to expose my hurts to heal others while supporting me in each step of this journey.

My siblings, Rob and Melissa, brother and sister-in-love, you keep my world in order weekly as I do what I love to do. Dad and Mom, you have always been there for my boys and me and always believed in me. I love you all!

INTRODUCTION

PAIN IS PART of life on earth. When we experience painful seasons, we often begin to question whether God still cares or if He even exists. But truth be told, many times we create our own storms. Then we get mad when it rains.

That's what I was doing. But after being twice married and divorced, losing my business, and having to move back in with my parents with my two boys in tow, I went on a journey to find God, myself, and my purpose. I chose to no longer blame everyone else for my situation, and instead, I gave God permission to heal my heart.

Let me tell you, heartbreak is no joke. After my divorce, when my heart felt as if it were breaking, my body literally ached day and night. Many nights I lay in bed, sobbing and begging God to take my pain from me. But He said, "I cannot take the pain. You must give it to Me."

From that moment on I became intentional about my healing and freedom. I realized God had entrusted me with pain. He had enrolled me in "life college," and I wouldn't owe a dime in student loans.

I was raised in a very strict denomination, and I always felt worthless, like the black sheep of the family. Therefore, it was easy for me to allow self-destructive behaviors to determine my future. But God used that painful season to change the trajectory of my entire life. Instead of taking me out, that crushing experience produced an anointing that would help pull others from hell's grip.

Pain is the prerequisite for promotion. I like to call these painful times the "cocoon experience" because they are dark, scary, and uncomfortable seasons. Nothing about them feels good, but their purpose is beautiful beyond human imagination.

**IF YOU HAVE A HEARTBEAT,
YOU HAVE A PURPOSE. DON'T GIVE UP!**
—*@RealTalkKim*

Seeing how God uses the cocoon experience in our lives is probably why I'm so amazed by the gorgeous butterflies that begin as caterpillars. The cocoon season is like no other. When God sends you there, He forces you to lose who you are so you can become who you are supposed to be. The cocoon is deceiving, and while you're in that place, you may be tempted to accept it as your new, permanent residence. In reality, the cocoon is only temporary, but it is a necessary part of your transformation.

Experiencing God's transforming grace is amazing, but the process doesn't always feel good. I know that painful seasons can be lonely times of frustration and identity crisis. You have a promise of your purpose from God, but your environment doesn't resemble that promise at all.

You have to trust what God is doing in the darkness and work with Him as He forms you. He is re-creating you through your pain. The dark time is not a sentence but a season. Philippians 1:6 says, "He who has begun a good work in you will complete it." Stop looking at the process, and keep your eyes on the promise.

Heartbreak, pain, and struggles are inevitable. What matters is how you play the cards you are dealt. Will you be a game changer or a benchwarmer? Will your pain be temporary or become permanent? Decide today: Are you going to nurse your wounds for the rest of your life? Or will you make the devil regret that he ever messed with you?

Determine that you are getting better and not bitter. Your pain is a setup for your promotion and purpose. What the devil meant for evil God is using for good. If you will allow Him, He will turn your scars into stars, your pain into your pulpit, and your mess into your message. God wants to take the bad that has happened to you and shift it for your good. God wants to transform your life, but you must cooperate with Him.

I want to help you move in a new direction instead of going back and repeating old cycles. But you're going to have to be intentional. You'll need to place a "Do not disturb" sign on your heart and allow God to heal every hurt area of your life.

That is what I did. *I had to do it.* My goal was to get unstuck from my past mistakes and move forward in Christ. I realized I had gone around my mountain of *self* far too many times. What I needed was to *decide* to allow God to make me whole.

Your healing is on the other side of the decision you make today. The only question is, Do you want to be made whole? (See John 5:1–6.) Only you can choose to access your freedom, take action, and release your purpose. If you do it, your bad and His good will collide in a place called purpose.

I invite you to take this healing journey with me and watch God restore all that you lost and more. Today I am married to an exceptional man of God. Together we share four amazing sons and four of the most beautiful grandchildren—all while pastoring the best church on the planet. I am privileged to travel weekly, sharing God's love with thousands of hurting people who are looking for change. I am a living witness of what happens when our bad meets His good.

**GOD WILL TURN YOUR SCARS INTO STARS,
YOUR PAIN INTO YOUR PULPIT,
AND YOUR MESS INTO YOUR MESSAGE.**
—*@RealTalkKim*

God has a plan for you too. I've been where you are, and I know what God will do if we put our lives in His hands. I declare that your future will be greater than your past. Are you ready to agree with me? Are you ready to believe that God is going to use your pain as a means of advancement in your life? Are you ready to have a shift in your mind? If so, take the next step with me, and let's discover how you ended up in this place.

PART I

HELP! I'M STUCK!

*It's time to own your truth and allow God
to turn your mess into a message!*

CHAPTER 1

WHAT HAPPENED?

WHETHER YOU LIVE a day, a month, or seventy-five years, you will experience pain and feel stuck in life with no way out. You might feel that way right now. Maybe a divorce has spun your life out of control. Until it happened to you, you could not imagine the emotional toll it would take on you, your children, and everyone near you.

Maybe your marriage is fine but you have lost a loved one. You feel as though you cannot move on or even picture your life going forward. It is hard to see past your pain and harder to believe it will ever go away.

Every day in ministry I encounter hurting people who have been abused by family members, assaulted by friends, and accused by virtual strangers. They feel stuck in their situations but dream of being free. They are part of a remnant that is begging for a new, healthy life in Christ Jesus.

That life is available, but first, my friend, you must identify and understand what brought you here.

LABEL IT

In my sermons I often talk about labels and how you don't have to accept the ones people give you. Yet so many people do because they want the unhealthy attention that goes with them.

Not all labels are negative. I was a preacher's kid, so

people assumed I had it all together. It was a label that could not have been further from the truth. I was jacked up and in a mess. For almost thirty-six years, I tried to fit in a world in which I was never comfortable.

Take my first marriage. I'm honestly not sure you can call it a marriage. We spent more time apart than together. My parents used to say that the wedding lasted longer than the marriage did. My second marriage lasted longer than my first, but it never thrived. In order to house and feed my family, I started an interior design business, which was an instant hit. To people on the outside, my life looked like a fairy tale. For sixteen years I sported designer labels, drove fancy cars, and lived in a gated community. Yet my marriage was a roller coaster, and the good days never overshadowed the toxic ones.

In both relationships my true identity was lost. I was called to be a butterfly but became a chameleon. In high school I was popular and had lots of friends, not because I fit in but because I stood out. Yet in marriage I compromised my identity to gain someone's love.

My second divorce nearly wrecked me, and it devastated my boys. Another attempt at marriage had failed. For months I lay in bed, sobbing and questioning God. Then somehow I decided to seek Him instead. I decided I would not allow my down season to define my lifetime. I was determined to get unstuck.

Like a turtle trudging through peanut butter, I made slow, but steady, progress. God had always wanted to heal me, but I had to let Him into my hurt places. He is a perfect gentleman and enters only when invited.

A woman in John chapter 4 discovered the power of letting Jesus into her pain. She'd had five husbands, and the man with whom she was living was not her spouse. Maybe he was the husband of another woman who lived nearby. I don't know, but I believe she was embarrassed and fearful of what others thought. Her integrity was compromised, and Jesus called her out on it—not to crush her but to make her whole.

Like many people today, this woman was stuck in a cycle of poor relationships. She could have stayed the way she was and settled for less than God wanted for her. But she reached out to Jesus, and one encounter with Him changed not only her life but her whole community when she began to share her testimony with the very people she once feared.

You might be stuck just like the woman in John 4, thinking your life will never change, but keep reading. By the time you finish this book, you can be walking in total freedom. But if instead of letting God into your hurt, you continue making poor decisions, you will find yourself unable to stop the bleeding. Everything you try will cost you more than you can afford to pay. That's how sin is. One season can cost you your spouse; another can cost you your job.

If you've been wondering what happened to the person God called you to be, you have to get to the bottom of what has you stuck in this season. No one arrives at her kingdom purpose by accident. I firmly believe that you attract not what you want but what you are. When you walk around thinking there is no hope, no joy, no answer, no better, and no light at the end of the tunnel, that is exactly what you get. You end up labeling yourself as a victim in your own story. But I already told you about labels. They are meant to be worn on shoes, clothes, and accessories, not people.

You do not have to be a victim or anything else people have called you. In school I was called *learning disabled*. If I had kept that label, you probably would not be reading this book right now.

LABELS ARE MEANT TO BE WORN ON SHOES,
CLOTHES, AND ACCESSORIES, NOT PEOPLE.
—*@RealTalkKim*

Do you feel labeled by where you are or what you have experienced? Are you in an abusive marriage? Were you sexually abused as a child? Do you feel stuck in moments from your past? You might even be suffering from survivor's remorse because everyone in your family was abused except you. Now you live with the guilt of having been spared the harm that befell them.

I remember wondering why I seemed to be the only one in my family who couldn't keep a marriage together. The devastation of divorce reached far beyond my ex and me. We signed on the line, but our entire family felt the pain, especially our boys. If you were abused or divorced, you know what I mean. It happened to you, but it touched everyone.

Painful experiences will brand us if we let them. Joseph's brothers labeled him a dreamer, but he was much more than that. Joseph was an interpreter of dreams and an intelligent and honorable young man. These qualities eventually landed him in Pharaoh's palace as his second in command. First, however, he was betrayed, presumed dead, falsely accused, imprisoned, and forgotten. (See Genesis chapters 37 and 39–50.)

Can you identify with any part of Joseph's story? I know I can.

I have been labeled, misunderstood, and accused. I was taught in church years ago that if you leave the stalk, you'll get peeled like a banana. But when my life fell apart, I couldn't figure out how to stay in a church that rejected broken vessels and forgot they were still in the potter's hands. After my second divorce, I was as good as dead to the religious world. As far as they were concerned, I had already secured my eternity in hell.

Yet mercy said *no*. God had a predestined future for me. I had to walk through hell, but it was so I could come out *on fire* and bring as many people as possible out with me.

No Job   Money   Car   Home

SIDE EFFECTS

Traumatic life experiences can produce a multitude of side effects. Have you seen those pharmaceutical ads that tout a drug's benefits and then rattle off a litany of horrible side effects? By the end of the ad, you'd rather live with the sickness than risk the reactions. But God's "medicine" is different. When you show Him the hurt, He reaches out to heal it. Your healing has already been purchased at Calvary. (See Isaiah 53:5 and 1 Peter 2:24.)

Family
Sickness
lost
death

Because the root causes of our hurts vary, our side effects are different too. Mine were anger, shame, and depression. The anger was directed mainly at myself. I felt I had to maintain the facade and make the marriage work, if only for my boys' sake. One reason I worked day and night to afford our lifestyle was that I could not give my boys the emotional support they needed. I lavished them with expensive gifts instead, which ultimately made me feel like a double failure.

My first divorce had been forgiven, but the humiliation of a second one seemed unsurvivable. My parents were well-known and respected pastors within our Christian organization. The doctrine was simple: if you get divorced, you will go to hell on a Slip 'N Slide. Not only was I divorced; I was penniless and moving back into my parents' home.

You probably know what came next: depression. Sadness overwhelmed me, and I lay in bed day after day rehearsing my ordeal. I replayed the final days, months, and years of the marriage to see what I could have done differently. As the memories rolled through my mind, my shame and anger intensified.

You might be where I was—overwhelmed by life's side

effects and in the fight of your life. Getting out of bed is a chore. All you want is a dark room and some more sleep. You feel protected with the covers pulled up over your ears. You want to shut out the crisis and the whole world. You have no motivation to begin another day because yesterday was called *disaster*. You are well aware that your decisions set up this avalanche of catastrophes, yet the side effects of life seem unbearable.

Yes I say this all the time

STUCK ON "WHY ME?"

I used to ask myself, "Did I behave badly in baby heaven?" I could not believe I was the one in my family and circle of friends who married twice before the age of twenty. I kept comparing my life with my brother's. He married his childhood sweetheart, and they are still married. I wondered, "Why couldn't I hold my marriage together?"

Each time I got married, I thought it would be forever. Who puts on a wedding dress thinking, "If this doesn't work out, I'll try again later"? No one wants a failed marriage. No one wants to be abused by a spouse, abandoned by a parent, or rejected by loved ones, either.

Three years into my second marriage, when everything was going wrong, I told my mom how determined I was to make it work. Even though I'd failed in my first marriage, I would do whatever it took to see the second one succeed.

WE SHOULD DO LESS PRAYING FOR GOD TO CHANGE THE SITUATION AND MORE PRAYING FOR HIM TO CHANGE US IN THE SITUATION.
—@RealTalkKim

yes

Expectations don't always go according to plan, however. Our decisions and life's little "accidents" sabotage them. Like Abraham and Sarah in the Old Testament, when we see nothing changing, we decide God must need our help.

So we create our Ishmaels, not realizing that God's timing is different from ours. When we look back later, shattered dreams and hopelessness are all we see. We cry out, "Why me?" and blame God for the storms we created out of our desperation for answers when He didn't "show up."

We hurt ourselves when we insist that God's deliverance must come in the package we prefer. Sometimes we look in one direction when He is coming from another angle, and we miss His answer, which is always perfect and always begins where our idea of perfection ends. That's why I believe we should do less praying for God to change the situation and more praying for Him to *change us in the situation*. That is the freedom we really need.

WHAT HAS YOU STUCK?

There are a lot of things that can cause us to get stuck. Sometimes we're stuck because we have not adequately dealt with old hurts. Therefore, we live in the past, holding grudges and making excuses for why we failed. But our blame shifting sets us up for even more failure. And when we blame others, we invite our difficult seasons to define the rest of our lives.

At other times we're stuck because we failed to anticipate what was coming. Most people at some point in their lives wonder, "What happened? How did I end up here?" Life has a way of catching us off guard and unprepared to deal with what it throws at us. We get so focused on completing our to-do lists and accomplishing our plans that the battle suddenly at hand practically takes our breath away.

It reminds me of when the flu virus hits. You start feeling achy and feverish, so you swallow some vitamins, eat chicken soup, and drink large quantities of orange juice to combat the bug. The response is good, but once you're feeling achy and feverish, it's too late. The virus is already in your system, and the doctor tells you it will have to run its course. So you're instructed to get some rest and drink plenty of fluids.

Some situations are like that flu. You can't avoid the crisis. You have to go through it. You have to face what has come at you because if you don't, it will crush you, and you will lose heart, lie down, and binge on fast food.

Our words can also cause us to get stuck. The Bible says, "Death and life are in the power of the tongue, and those who love it will eat its fruit" (Prov. 18:21). Your words can turn your life upside down, positively or negatively. It's easy to gripe about the struggle when you feel stuck. It is hard to find joy and peace when you are worried about the house payment or groceries for your family. But how you speak about a situation can determine how long you stay in it. The children of Israel wandered around in the desert for forty years because they chose to gripe and complain rather than praise God for delivering them from bondage and preparing a lush land they could call their own. (See Numbers 14:26–34.) Your words matter, and they affect you.

Other people's words can affect you too. When friends speak in faith jargon and expect you to make an immediate change, they can leave you feeling even worse. You think, "How can they know how I feel? What do they know about what I'm facing? They're not walking in my shoes." When they tell you to suck it up, you want to break their legs and tell them to walk it off.

DON'T LET YOUR MOUTH GET YOU IN TROUBLE. HOW YOU SPEAK ABOUT A SITUATION CAN DETERMINE HOW LONG YOU STAY IN IT.
—@RealTalkKim

When you're feeling stuck and walking through a season when it seems God is nowhere to be found, thoughts like that can come a mile a minute. It gets easier to stay in bed on Sundays than to sit in church with the Sunday Christians whose lives happen to be easier than yours. Sure, they can testify about God's goodness toward them, but could they have endured the loss, pain, and rejection you have suffered? Would they even be in church if they were locked in your circumstances?

The problem with these thoughts running through your mind is that they will eventually come out of your mouth and into your actions. You might not realize it, but you are prophesying doom over yourself. Your life cannot help but become what you have spoken. You will even surround yourself with people who look and act just like you.

Take a good look at your five closest friends. They represent what your life will be, and they are prophesying into your future. Take inventory of who is in your world. You might need to unfollow some people. Some who are in your life's VIP section need to be escorted to the upper balcony and told to watch you from a distance. I'm not being ugly; I'm talking about self-love.

Maybe family issues have you stuck. Were you raised in a household where dysfunction was the norm? Then there is probably some dysfunction around you now. Why? Because you don't know how to break the cycle. You are so familiar with deprivation and pain that you accept whatever you are handed. You don't feel worthy of anything else.

Maybe your family had low expectations for you or enabled your poor choices, never challenging you to be greater or do greater. Perhaps you were raised in a single-parent household and never saw healthy parental interaction. Maybe you never had a father to love you appropriately or show you how a woman should be treated in a healthy relationship. Maybe no one showed you how to be a faithful husband or a good father.

Generational curses are real, but generational blessings are real too. We have the power to change our trajectories by becoming intentional. That means choosing to live abundantly because we are free to change our minds. We can say, "No, I will not allow my past to be my future. I will not allow my DNA to control me. God is my DNA." (My dad has always said that DNA is our *divine nature attribute*. Even in my worst times I believed him.)

The issue you face might be physical. Maybe your weight is spiraling upward, and when you admit that you are scared, a friend says, "Hey, no one said life was going to be easy." (Isn't that what some "comforters" say as they "console" you?)

It is easy to tell people, "Suck it up. Everybody has problems." However, the issues are not always that simple. Maybe you went through seasons of emotional eating to cover your pain. Before you knew it, your behavior became chronic, and the food that once comforted you became a source of regret. It never healed your pain, and now you must deal with the aftereffects of overindulgence on your overall health.

Maybe you are dealing with heartbreak because someone you trusted turned around and broke you. You gave that person the most precious part of yourself, and he or she betrayed it. Now you find yourself paralyzed by pain so deep that you can't eat or sleep, and even your fingers ache.

We are human. We want answers. We want to know why those certain someones don't love us anymore. We wonder what we could have done differently. We think about it twenty-four hours a day. If they would just explain what the problem is, we could fix it and make life like it was before. That's what we want because we can't imagine living without that person.

Or have you perhaps allowed addictions to rule you because you "needed something" in the middle of the night? The house was quiet and peaceful to other family members, but you found no rest for the weary. Or are you wrestling with a diagnosis? What if the doctor's report is true? What if you have to take medication for the rest of your life or are given poor chances for tomorrow? How do you handle that?

Become intentional. Bring God into your situation. Determine that because He is the supreme physician, the doctor's diagnosis will not rule you. Remind yourself that when He heals and restores you, you will be better than you were before.

And if that miracle seems to take awhile to manifest, remember where God is. He's right there in the middle of your pain. I can tell you through experience that God uses our darkest seasons to catapult us into our greater days.

PAIN IS A TEACHER

Difficult seasons can make us feel out of control. We want the pain to go away, but what we really need is to learn from these times. It's not always about praying for God to change the situation; sometimes we need to ask Him to change us.

Without the pain you would never discover how strong you are. What the devil meant for evil God is using for your good. You might think you are hitting rock bottom, but you are discovering who the rock at the bottom is. It's Jesus!

Whatever has you stuck, get real with yourself and understand that if you are still alive, God isn't done with you yet. There is hope that your latter days will be greater than any you have lived so far. What you are going through won't last forever. How you see and walk through the situation can change everything. Complain, and you will remain. Praise, and you will come out a victor instead of a victim. God gave you praise as a weapon, but it's up to you to use it.

You might not like where you are, but this isn't the end of the line. You might not be OK today, tomorrow, next month, or even next year, but one thing is certain: God is in control.

YOU MIGHT THINK YOU ARE HITTING ROCK BOTTOM, BUT YOU ARE DISCOVERING WHO THE ROCK AT THE BOTTOM IS. IT'S JESUS!
—*@RealTalkKim*

The apostle Paul said, "What then shall we say to these things? If God is for us, who can be against us?" (Rom. 8:31). If you believe God is for you, act as though He is. I know this sounds overly simple. I can hear you thinking, "That's easier said than done." That is true. But to reach the place you would rather be, you must first *see it* and *believe it*. See the good future God is preparing for you, and believe it will become a reality!

I have experienced some intense challenges in my life, most of which I brought on myself. But some were strictly from the enemy. He was trying to take me out. He knew that if I got my act together, I would become a force to be reckoned with, and He was right. The devil never fights us because we are weak and feeble. He fights us because we are powerful.

You are strong! On the day you were born, the doctors heard your first cry, but hell heard your purpose. The devil recognized a game changer, a world challenger, a righteous warrior, and a hope dealer. That is why you feel as if you can't get a break.

Do not buy into victimhood. Refuse to concentrate on what is going wrong. Instead, focus your mind and renew it with God's Word. When you remind yourself of what God says about you and the promises He made to His people, you will start seeing yourself free instead of stuck. That is what happened to the woman who touched the hem of Jesus' garment.

> Suddenly, a woman who had a flow of blood for twelve years came from behind and touched the hem of His garment. For she said to herself, "If only I may touch His garment, I shall be made well." But Jesus turned around, and when He saw her He said, "Be of good cheer, daughter; your faith

has made you well." And the woman was made well from that hour.

—MATTHEW 9:20–22

We tend to talk about this woman's healing miracle but not her other miracle: she bled for twelve years and survived! She saw numerous doctors and gave up her life savings to get well. She must have been frail, yet she pressed her way through the crowd in order to touch Jesus' garment. It's a miracle that she survived twelve years to reach that day!

You might be dealing with issues in your body. Think about the woman with the issue of blood. She had no friends to carry her to Jesus. No doctor would make a house call. She burned through her cash and had nowhere else to go.

Have you hit your bottom? Are you trying to reach out one last time for an answer, praying that God will show you how to change your life? Is this another last-ditch attempt to take hold of the answer that always seems to be just beyond your grasp?

Here is the truth: God has a plan to do you good and not harm—to give you a future and a hope. On your road to recovery, praise Him for sustaining you! You *are* one step away from your miracle.

There was a young lady in our church who went through a season of grief and disappointment. When her father suffered a stroke, she was called away to handle his affairs. Although he was her birth dad, he had never played an active role in her life, yet she stepped in to assist with whatever he needed at the time. Watching her stop her world just to sit at his bedside was incredible. For almost a month she slept in waiting rooms and stayed with relatives as she assisted him during that season.

As she served her father during his illness, unresolved pain, loneliness, and feelings of abandonment began to surface. Through her service she was seeking some type of stabilization and an assurance that her family cared. Even when she returned home after dealing with this crisis, the longing for acceptance and belonging remained. But so much had changed while she was gone, she felt like an outsider.

Her friends had become busy with new ventures, and even in church so many new people were being added weekly in the midst of revival, she felt as though she were the visitor in a new congregation. Developing new relationships did not help. Instead of pushing her toward breakthrough, they inadvertently moved her toward breakdowns. No matter how she tried to recover from the lingering feelings of rejection and abandonment, she never experienced real restoration—until she decided to get unstuck.

> **GOD ISN'T IGNORING YOU;**
> **HE'S PREPARING YOU.**
> —*@RealTalkKim*

yes!

Determined to exit her funk and discover who God called her to be, she got involved in our church's recovery program for anyone with hurts, habits, and hang-ups. It took a minute for her to pull out of that dark season, but when she experienced breakthrough, it was an amazing victory. She was able to turn her mess into a message and has just recently completed her first book. Now she walks in a freedom unlike anything anyone would have imagined.

God did in this woman's life what I preach about every single day. She is proof that your down seasons don't have to define your future. If you will just face your heartbreak and admit that you are stuck, God can begin to move. All He needs is for you to acknowledge where you are and decide that it is time for change.

God isn't ignoring you; He's preparing you.

Before you move on to the next chapter, use the following

prayer to speak life over yourself and declare God's Word over your future.

> *Father, thank You for showing up and showing out in my life. Thank You for never giving up on me. Thank You for Your hand of blessing on my life. Expose the areas of my life—my thoughts and painful memories—that have caused me to become stuck. Today I choose to be free. In Jesus' name, amen.*

I DECLARE

I decree and declare over my life that what happened in the past no longer defines me.

The past will no longer define me. I am healed and have forgiveness to those who hurt and abandon me. I stepping out on faith and taking one step forward to Our Father God

Amen

CHAPTER 2

KILL THE WEEDS

YOU HAVE TAKEN your first step toward victory. You have discovered that you are stuck, and you want to uncover the reason. You realize that God never intended for you to just exist. He created you to live abundantly. You have identified some of the decisions that have kept you moving from one crisis to another. You also realize that in some cases you were not to blame for what happened.

This is huge. You are ready to face the issues that have tormented you and held you hostage. You are ready to be honest with yourself and admit that you have hung on to past hurts and rejection. You understand that it's time to let them go. You are tired of carrying the extra baggage you've accumulated through the years. You now want to focus on getting free. To do that, you'll have to start paying attention to your heart.

The Bible says in Proverbs 4:23 to protect your heart because everything you do flows from it. You might think the negative words you heard at home, in school, or among friends didn't hurt you. But if your thoughts keep going back to the degrading things people have said over the years and their words have left you feeling "less than," that clearly isn't true.

To find that place of healing, you must look deep within and be honest with the person in the mirror. It is easy to develop facades and adopt identities based on what others have said about you, but this will cause you to lose sight of who you really are, and it will keep you from becoming the person God created you to be.

SOMETIMES A HEARTBREAK SHAKES YOU AWAKE AND HELPS YOU SEE THAT YOU ARE WORTH MORE THAN WHAT YOU WERE SETTLING FOR.
—@RealTalkKim

You may have heard that knowledge is power. God said in Hosea 4:6 that His people were destroyed because of a lack of knowledge. He didn't say the problem was the enemy. He said the problem was what they did not know. So why do we give the enemy credit for every challenge we face? Why do we always make it about the devil? The enemy cannot destroy you unless you let him. The devil knows who you are, even if you've been living behind a mask. He knows you were born to be a threat to his kingdom, and he wants to keep you from becoming the person you were created to be. So he sends distractions to get you focused on everything but God.

Knowledge is power.

DISTRACTIONS

Distractions sneak up on us. Today I can see several reasons I kept circling my heap of chaos and confusion. I wouldn't listen to my parents, I was a rebel, and I insisted on learning through experience. I actually believed I knew what was best for me.

As a teenager, I told myself, "If a man ever lays a hand on me, I will take a frying pan to him." It was a very different story when I was living in the middle of a chaotic situation. The enemy was already plotting to take me out through distractions. If he could entangle me in a fight for my life, he could dissuade me from helping others. In my rebellion I abetted him and found myself in a dysfunctional marriage that was wrecking my life.

I wondered, "How in the world did I get here?" I felt so rejected and unprotected by some of the most important people in my life. Little did I know that I had entered a six-year downward spiral. I tried hard to keep my family together, especially for the sake of my sons. But after a while it felt as if every promise made was broken. The enemy even convinced me that I deserved all the negative things that were happening to me.

So instead of being transparent, I muted myself, never telling a soul what was going on. I mechanically arose day after day to do what I did so well: make my clients' homes beautiful. No one knew about the hurt or the rejection. At one point I sat on my bed, weeping and asking God, "Where are You? How did I get here?"

My life didn't resemble anything I had envisioned as a little girl. There was no white picket fence, and there were none of the rainbows and butterflies I expected from marriage. I believe my stuckness was due in part to my legalistic background in the church. I was raised in a denomination that rejected women preachers and used women to model their rules. So while men in our denomination seemed to step out of *GQ* magazine, their wives wore no makeup or jewelry and were not permitted to cut their hair.

When I was in middle school, I felt like an ugly duckling. It seemed as if everything I wanted to do with my hair or clothes was met with a big fat *no*. Everyone at church looked angry, sad, or miserable. My dad was a pastor, and we were in church all the time. Even at about six years of age I watched the choir sing about God's goodness and thought, "If they are all going to heaven, why do they look so unhappy? If I have to spend eternity with them, I don't want to go."

I decided I wanted to be different, but I had no idea how

much the trajectory of my life would shift. It was unlike anything my parents had imagined for me!

WEEDS AND WEIGHTS

If you ever felt as if school was a struggle you could not handle, I understand. Every day of high school was a struggle for me. My brother breezed through accelerated classes, while I fought to retain even a little of what I learned.

My brother and I were worlds apart scholastically. He had no idea how frustrated I was or how I compared myself with him every day. Even as far back as the second grade, I wondered why my life was so unbearable. Every morning I would scream and cry because I didn't want to go to school. My mom had to wrestle me out of the car and into school.

After months of this I finally opened up and told the principal what I was facing in the classroom. Whenever I struggled to read a certain word, my teacher would speak sharply and embarrass me in front of my classmates. She had twenty students to think about, so she certainly could not spend precious time with one struggling student. Telling the principal was a good thing for me to do, but it didn't bring any real change. I realize now that I never understood the principle of phonics, so I did not get the foundation needed to just pick up a book and enjoy the read. I now see this is the reason that, while my family could read for hours, I would often flip through magazines.

In the second grade I was tested for a learning disability, and it was determined that I needed special tutoring. At first, when the teacher announced dismissal of the "special kids" for one-on-one tutoring, I walked out feeling like a VIP. Then one day during my sixth-grade year my teacher casually announced dismissal for the students with learning disabilities. I was brokenhearted. That casual statement immediately released an avalanche of mental confusion and self-judgment. That slip of the tongue led to a long season of feeling unworthy.

I realized I was nothing like my successful parents or even my brother. I was that child who looked happy on the outside but was weary inside from struggling to be what the world expected me to be. My parents were successful as pastors, so all the kids at my church desired to be a part of our family. I always heard, "Kim, you have the perfect family, the perfect home." Yet I was anything but perfect. I didn't know why I couldn't do something as simple as remember the spelling words for my test on Friday. I wondered why I had been created so stupid.

Looking back, I realize that the enemy was distracting me even then with self-esteem problems. He did it because he wanted to thwart the plans of God for my life so that when I hit my forties, I wouldn't be writing books and assisting my friends in their deliverance. *But God!*

We all have stories like this. Out of embarrassment, we hide them and never share how we overcame and succeeded. When we keep our hurt and rejection secret, our hearts become sad. Instead of believing we are "fearfully and wonderfully made" (Ps. 139:14), we hide behind masks. Over time pain is woven into the fabric of our beings.

The fruit of hurt and rejection manifests differently in each of our lives. It reminds me of the variety of weeds that sprout overnight in a groomed yard. My homeowners' association polices our neighborhood to make sure all lawns are mowed and all hedges are trimmed. I left on a trip one day as our yard guy was mowing our lawn. When I returned two days later, I was shocked. It looked as if the lawn had not been cared for in a week. Three-inch-tall weeds had appeared virtually overnight.

I realized that the weeds had root systems hidden underground. The systems had matured enough to produce hundreds of plants in a couple of days.

It made me think about the people who ask me how to release the bondages that keep them imprisoned. They want to know how to handle their "weeds"—their toxic relationships, addictions, abuse, adultery, depression, and fear. They make life changes yet gradually return to the familiar things that keep them wounded and lost. Even oppression and abandonment can be familiar and easy to go back to. I know this because I lived it. I went around my mountains of fear, doubt, and depression years longer than I imagined I would.

The day I returned to hundreds of weeds that seemed to have grown in my lawn overnight, I received such a simple revelation: those weeds were an example of the way sin manifests in our lives. On the outside we look as though we are walking by faith and growing spiritually day by day. Yet on the inside our sin nature is allowed to become a mature root system that eventually wreaks havoc.

When we allow those weeds to grow, they choke off the grass that should be growing in the lawn and keep us distracted from God's purpose. We need to recognize what is really going on. The devil keeps bringing up the past because he wants to derail the success that is in our future.

As I mentioned previously, even in your premature, underdeveloped state the enemy can see who you are. He's not trying to kill you; he's trying to kill the deliverer in you. He's not after who you are now but who you are going to be. He knows he can't take you out, so he tries to wear you out. He doesn't want you to have enough energy to chase after God. He wants you to lose faith in what God has promised you.

**THE DEVIL'S NOT TRYING TO KILL YOU;
HE'S TRYING TO KILL THE DELIVERER IN YOU.**
—*@RealTalkKim*

It's a shame when the enemy sees more potential in us than we see in ourselves! How sad it is that we get weighed down and weary. Each weekend as I fly, I have to limit the weight of my luggage. If I pack five extra pounds, the airline charges me astronomically. Airlines do it because weight overages affect flight safety and fuel efficiency.

Imagine what baggage from your past will cost! The enemy would love for you to carry unforgiveness, bitterness, anger, and resentment that turn into hatred and eat away at your soul the way weeds eat away at your lawn.

You may have been under this kind of attack for so long that you have lost hope and can't see a way out. I'm here to remind you that if you stay committed, God will take you from glory to glory. I'm not playing with the devil. I am serious. In the name of Jesus, I declare that every knee must bow. Satan has no defense against the Word of God. He has no choice but to withdraw in defeat. This is why it is so important to stay focused and not get distracted. You must cooperate with God for your healing and breakthrough.

All this time you have been thinking that God has forgotten you and is angry with you. No! Even though God seems silent in this season, He is doing a mighty work in and through you. Do you remember test days at school? Your teacher walked around the room very quietly. When you raised your hand to ask questions, he or she wouldn't let you because you were being tested.

It's the same with your heavenly Father. In your testing season He does not always speak, because in the silence you discover who you are. Difficult times have a way of showing us what's in us. We discover how strong we are when we live through pain.

Challenges make you stronger. While I was in high school, my grandparents moved in with us. As pastors, my parents were frequently called upon to speak at funerals. My mom would always tell me that she could not imagine releasing her parents to death. She would weep as she comforted others, knowing that one day she would face the same loss.

After my grandfather's passing, I asked my mother how she had the strength to speak at his funeral. She explained that it was because of the powerful presence of the Holy Spirit. The Lord had always been her comfort, but until she walked through the pain of loss, she hadn't experienced the depths of that comfort. In her grief she felt an overwhelming peace that everything would be all right.

The storms you fear reveal your strength. So rest easy and travel light! Let go of old habits and toxic friends. Don't let the fear of being alone keep you in a negative flow. Take a step back. Assess where you have been and what you have accomplished. If you are allowing others to determine your position in life, you are preventing your heavenly Father from being your Lord.

Friends cannot determine your success. That is why *you* are fearfully and wonderfully made. They may be able to enjoy the fruit of your labor, but they cannot determine your path unless you let them. Root out the insecurity, manipulation, and codependency that have held you back. Let God bring direction to your life.

> Therefore we also, since we are surrounded by so great
> a cloud of witnesses, let us lay aside every weight,
> and the sin which so easily ensnares us, and let us
> run with endurance the race that is set before us.
> —HEBREWS 12:1

The verse tells us to "lay aside *every* weight." When faith and doubt war in your spirit, follow God's instruction in 2 Corinthians 10:5: "[Cast] down arguments and every high thing that exalts itself against the knowledge of God, bringing every thought into captivity to the obedience of Christ." The devil will try to sit on one shoulder and tell you what you can't do, remind you how people have wronged you in the past, remind you of your age, and tell you about the money you lack to do what God told you to do. But if God told you to do it, He will bring you through it. If He tells you to return to school, apply for a promotion, or get a larger apartment, then let Him help you. It is when you approach a situation with doubt that your God potential is strangled.

Unbelief is a manifestation of distrust and uncertainty. It will have you sure about yourself and your future one minute and tearing yourself down the next. You reach a faith high on Sunday morning and shout all over the church, but on your way to your car the devil taunts, "Yeah, *but...!*"

Cast down that imagination and decide which root system will be evident in your life—faith and trust, or fear and doubt. Determine what will proceed from your mouth. Choose the words that support a life of consistency, obedience, diligence, and faith. Then let the fruit of your faith walk be made manifest. Declare that God is Lord over every situation, and let His ways guide the decisions that determine your position.

When you kill the future-stealing "weeds" that manipulate you and distract from your purpose, you can focus on what is good, holy, pure, and righteous. Imprisoned and in shackles, the apostle Paul still did God's bidding and gave us an authoritative word that empowers us to break out of our bondages. Destined to die for the gospel's sake, he set an example of trust and certainty in the face of death. He wrote:

> Finally, brethren, whatever things are true, whatever things are noble, whatever things are just, whatever things are pure, whatever things are lovely, whatever things are of good report, if there is any virtue

and if there is anything praiseworthy—meditate on these things. The things which you learned and received and heard and saw in me, these do, and the God of peace will be with you.

—Philippians 4:8–9

Those who work hard to bring you down will watch as God takes you up. Keep feeding on His Word, and the carnality that once worked toward your demise will be cut off at the root. It is time to quit blaming people, places, and situations for where you are today. Just know that if you are still breathing, God is not finished with you yet. Continue to walk out your freedom by letting go of hurts and unforgiveness, and allowing God to feed your spirit.

As you take this journey, ask God to send you someone who will hold you accountable for your decisions and actions. This needs to be a godly person with whom you can take off the mask and reveal your true self, a wise and spiritually mature person who won't judge you but will hold you up in prayer, challenge you, and ask you the tough questions. Your healing is on the other side of your revealing.

**IF YOU ARE STILL BREATHING,
GOD IS NOT FINISHED WITH YOU YET.**
—@RealTalkKim

Shout, "It's time for my elevation!" That is God's amazing compensation plan for your life.

Heavenly Father, thank You for keeping my heart open as You get to the bottom of my junk. I humbly come before You, giving You all that I am. I choose to trust that You are working behind the scenes on my behalf. Thank You for being my Deliverer and my healing source through every season of my life. I am excited for what You are doing in and through me. I am open to Your will, and I know Your provision is there for me through every step of this journey. In Jesus' name, amen.

I DECLARE

I decree and declare over myself and all who are connected to me a release of anointing to break and destroy every yoke. I release a spirit of love, power, and a sound mind over myself right now. I walk in total victory and blessings. My best days are the rest of my days.

With everything I've been through I'm still breathing with a smile (most of the time)

Like Nemo

Just keeping breathing and recieving Gods grace

CHAPTER 3

ONE DECISION AWAY

CHANGE BEGINS IN your mind with a decision to let God transform you and your current situation. You can't do it alone. You need God's help. He wants you to enjoy a better life, stronger relationships, and victory in Him.

Change requires a new direction. It means moving away from unwise decisions and the situations those decisions created. Change demands your agreement to change. When you agree to wanting and needing change, you think in new ways. This new thinking then inspires new actions.

I am no stranger to change. In 2006 I felt lost and hopeless and changed my entire life. It was messy. I was still angry at God for not intervening or healing my marriage. Lying in bed one night, I yelled at God. "If You won't heal my marriage, You can at least take away this pain!"

I sensed Him telling me, "I can't take the pain from you. You must release it to Me."

That night I realized that God required my cooperation. He wasn't my genie in a bottle. It was up to me to change my mind. A better life would start when I chose it.

A friend of mine has been diagnosed with lung cancer. For years everyone who cares about him begged him to quit smoking. Instead, he would put his oxygen tank on his shoulder and walk outside for another smoke.

Five days after his cancer diagnosis, I visited him and asked, "Have you quit smoking?"

He told me he had not smoked for five days. I was not shocked because I have seen this story before. People wait until there seems to be no choice and no hope before they decide to move on. They don't change until they are ready to change. Sometimes a cancer diagnosis gets them ready.

You might be where my friend was. You have awakened to the reality that your world stinks and it's time to change. Being angry at God has solved nothing, so you try getting your life in order instead. Weary from fighting constant battles, you are ready to take back everything the devil has stolen from you. You know that playing the victim is doing you no good. Complaining is not changing anything. Stalking people on social media and comparing yourself to others are not changing anything.

Am I describing your situation? If so, you are in a place where real change can begin. Let go of the people, places, and things that no longer fit your life and calling. You can outgrow people just like you outgrow clothes. There's no use forcing relationships to continue past their expiration dates. Sticking with the wrong people suppresses your growth and your future.

DON'T LET SOMEONE DIM YOUR LIGHT
SIMPLY BECAUSE IT'S SHINING IN THEIR EYES.
—@RealTalkKim

Letting your down seasons define your lifetime also suppresses your future. That is exactly what I did with my failures. Instead of seeing them as my "life college," I tried stabilizing what God wanted to remove from my life. I was so stubborn and independent that when God dealt with me spiritually, I inhibited His will. I was like the prodigal son in Luke 15:11–32. He left his father's house with his inheritance yet eventually returned home, broken and penniless, when he came to the end of himself, his will, his desires, and his plans. That's how it was with me. I could not receive God's mercy and His purpose for my life until I was willing to release that stubbornness and independent spirit. Thank God, I finally became honest with myself.

DON'T SETTLE FOR A LITTLE BIT

God informed me that my unforgiveness toward certain people was another reason I was stuck. I was so busy trying to teach them a lesson that I was missing my blessings. Honestly I thought I was free from unforgiveness. Then I realized what my problem was: I was so comfortable with deprivation and pain that tiny slivers of forgiveness made me feel as if I was whole.

God warned me not to abort the healing He had in store. I think many of us do that. We experience a release in one area, take partial steps toward forgiveness, and drop some of our baggage. The healing is incomplete, but our depression no longer seems to smother us. When your pain is widespread, the slightest relief feels like an enormous breakthrough. So we move on, getting ahead of God and aborting real wholeness.

During my divorce I was so stuck in a place of partial healing and forgiveness that I told God, "I'm thirty-seven years old and not getting any younger. I need You to hurry up with this healing process. I don't want to be old and searching for a husband. If You don't hurry it up, I'll check out some dating sites."

I was three years into my healing journey and had yet to recognize my fear of being alone. I had always looked for someone to satisfy needs that only God could fill. Now I was doing it again. Because I wanted to control my life, I tried getting ahead of God. He reminded me how that habit was largely responsible for what I disliked about my life.

Right then and there I made a decision to get out of His way and endure the healing process, however long it took. Today I realize that there is a "God-shaped hole" in the soul of every human being. Nothing can satisfy us like the love of God. When we have ironclad expectations of how life is supposed to look, we get bitter (and stuck) when our lives don't look exactly that way.

We have to take inventory and understand where we are so we can see the healing process clearly and stay committed to it. After all, what we want more than anything is to be whole.

YOU MUST CHOOSE TO BE CONTENT

Do you lack contentment? Do you compare yourself with others and wonder why they seem to be more blessed, happier, more peaceful, and more, more, more of everything you desire? Paul said in Philippians 4:11 that whatever his situation was, he had learned to be content. If an apostle and one of the most educated men of his time allowed his circumstances to educate him, we can too.

Contentment is not something you find. It is something you decide. You must choose to keep challenges from dictating your attitude. Paul said to invite contentment by thinking about things that are pure, just, noble, lovely, and of good report. (See Philippians 4:8.) Your thoughts shape your attitude, and your attitude determines your altitude in life.

Do you see your glass as half empty or half full? Something on the inside is framing what you see on the outside. The changes you desire also come from within. When you allow the Holy Spirit to work on you from within, you become a victor instead of a victim, even if your external circumstances seem unchanged. Notice I did not choose the word *survivor* but *victor*. A survivor just makes it through a battle alive. A victor not only wins the war but continues to slay his giants. You cannot become a victor without going through something. "The righteous person may have many troubles, but the LORD delivers him from them all" (Ps. 34:19, NIV).

YOUR ATTITUDE DETERMINES YOUR ALTITUDE IN LIFE.
—@RealTalkKim

To move out of discontentment, you need to remember who your Deliverer is. Let the Lord address your troubles. Allow Him to be your buffer during the storms that come your way—and they *will* come. Everyone has ups and downs. It is easy to make comparisons, especially when you are struggling and your friends' jobs, marriages, and children are looking good. But everyone hurts at some point, and life is never fair.

If you are breathing, you will face difficulty. The psalmist David knew how unfair life could be. God had anointed David to be king of Israel. Yet King Saul, whom God rejected, stalked David because of jealousy. Though he was persecuted on his way to the throne, David continued to be loyal to King Saul, who was not loyal and considered David his enemy. While David ran for his life and hid in caves, he learned that God was his only source. He trusted God, writing, "The steps of a good man are ordered by the LORD, and He delights in his way. Though he fall, he shall not be utterly cast down; for the LORD upholds him with His hand" (Ps. 37:23–24).

To move toward forgiveness and contentment, you must believe and know that God is *the* Deliverer. No matter what you are facing, God has promised to deliver you. He doesn't say in Psalm 34:17 that He will deliver you from *some* of your struggles as long as you do everything perfectly and never complain, doubt, or fear. No. He says that if you believe in Him and give Him residency in your heart, He will deliver you from *all* your troubles.

THE DEVIL MAY BE WHISPERING IN YOUR EAR,
"YOU ARE NOT STRONG ENOUGH TO WITHSTAND THIS STORM."
GO ON AND WHISPER BACK, "I AM THE STORM!"
—*@RealTalkKim*

When you receive Jesus as your Lord and Savior and accept His forgiveness, you know for certain that He is working in your life, even when you cannot see Him. You trust Him when you cannot trace His footsteps. You understand that He will deliver you again. You believe that when He stepped off His throne and onto the cross, He did it for you.

Jesus went to the cross to make salvation available for anyone who would receive it. But if you had been the only person on the planet, He would have died just for you. You are so important to Him that He would have taken thirty-nine stripes just for you. He would have died and said, "It is finished," just for you. Nothing you could do would make Him love you any more or less. All of you is precious to Him.

Even before you were a reality in your mother's womb, God validated you. How awesome is that? He already knew every mistake you would make, even that abortion in your high school years. He knew that your dad would not be the loving father you needed and you would end up looking for love in all the wrong places. He knew about that husband you would chase away with your ranting. He knew you would do that because you were afraid of letting anyone get close enough to hurt you again.

God knew before the foundation of the world that the walls you built to protect your heart would keep out your blessings. He knew that you would become a career student, working for multiple degrees in order to win your parents' approval, which you would never receive. He knew you would end up overqualified, underemployed, and unable to pay off your college loans.

God knew all this before it happened, and He still

validated you. He even knew that you would read this book one day. He saw you experiencing an awakening that would empower you to walk away from your past and into your future.

Some of us have been lost in ugly feelings of unworthiness and discontentment for so long that instead of allowing ourselves the abundance of God's grace, we punish ourselves. We overlook the richness of our experiences, forgetting that every season is part of a best-selling story God is weaving together. We have a say in the outcome and are just one decision away from transformation. Let's quit trying to right our wrongs and let them go instead.

I'm talking to you as plainly as I know how. You can decide right now to stop living out of your life's rearview mirror and start seeing clearly through the windshield. It's right in front of you.

LET IT GO

As my world fell into a million jagged pieces, I had a decision to make. I could become pitiful and let the shattering define my future, or I could see those fragments as the beautifully broken parts of a mosaic that was coming together. If I allowed it, those pieces would welcome the light and, like many tiny prisms, reveal its colors.

Beautifully broken is where God does His best work. Think of a disco ball. When it revolves, it makes an entire room sparkle *because* it is made of many broken pieces of glass. That is how God's healing power works through us. Ministry comes out of our broken places. God uses people with the worst pasts to create the best futures. He uses those who were shattered, tattered, and torn to heal other people.

It is so important for us to stop trying to impress people and start being effective for God. We have to realize that

He will never let what we lost be the best we ever have. Our best is yet to come, if we are willing to change.

GOD USES PEOPLE WITH THE WORST PASTS
TO CREATE THE BEST FUTURES.
—@RealTalkKim

When I found myself getting divorced and realized I was losing my marriage, business, home, and dignity, I had to be gut-level honest with myself. Success was gone from the picture. I just needed to survive and get a job. My interior design business was lost, and I was too emotionally scarred to even think of starting over.

I wondered what God was doing, and I felt as if He were totally punking me. I cannot tell you how many times I shouted at Him. I wanted to understand what was happening and why. Looking back, I expected Him to just take care of me, not let me suffer. I was a preacher's kid, raised in church. So what happened? How could I have ended up in such devastation?

Everything was still about me. I thought the whole world revolved around Kimberly and her needs. In retrospect, I realize that He was turning my mess into a message. He knew I didn't like people. He also knew that where He was taking me, I would need to do more than like people; I'd need to *love* them.

At the time, I was working in a department store and was angry and embarrassed to be earning minimum wage. Because my character needed work, I was afraid people would ridicule me. So God used my setbacks to build my character. I learned that I could not allow what people thought of me to distract me from what I knew about myself. God was using the situation to deliver me from people.

Are you stuck there? People pleasing will totally keep you

stuck because you care more about what people think than what God does. That can't lead you anyplace good!

God showed me my self-righteousness and my need for approval. Gradually I learned to take my eyes off people and things and get out of my feelings. He showed me that anytime I allowed other people's opinions to rule my decisions, pride was involved. Proverbs 16:18 says, "Pride goes before destruction, and a haughty spirit before a fall." I thought I was suffering from embarrassment or insecurity, but I was wrong; it was pride. Pride is what caused me to put on my facade each day and let the world think everything was OK. I wanted them to think I was being blessed, while inside I was falling apart.

To become free, you have to be honest with who you are and what you have allowed in your life. If you are repeating endless cycles of distrust, manipulation, and dishonesty, and if you keep inviting the same types of broken people into your world, it is time to let honesty be your best friend. Ask yourself hard questions. "Why can't I keep a job? Why is my personal life always full of drama? Why am I the common denominator in all of it?"

No one likes hearing the cold, hard facts. It is so much easier to blame others than to own the truth. Out of love, however, I am compelled to tell you the truth: until you are willing to face that beautiful person in the mirror and let go of the brokenness that keeps you stuck, *nothing will ever change.* You will spend a fortune on therapists but find no cure. You will perpetuate the patterns that contaminate everyone and everything around you. You will wear yourself to a frazzle.

It's just not worth it! You are so much more valuable to God than you realize. Instead of thinking about how hard it is to change, think of how much better your life will be when you get free.

While we're on the subject of letting go, think about who gets credit for your situation. When you are hurting, it is tempting to blame the enemy for whatever goes wrong. Without thinking, you say, "The enemy is trying to take my car. It overheated today."

No. The devil can't drive. You just need an oil change.

"The devil is trying to take my marriage."

No. He doesn't want your spouse. He can't even get married. Stop giving him credit for every negative experience you have. It is your responsibility to address the drama in your life. Instead of getting on social media and telling everyone you are purging your friends list because you are done with the drama, admit that *you are the drama*. When you get healed, you won't need to stir up that mess. When you are healed, you want to bring people into your peace, not your pieces.

LET IT HURT, LET IT BLEED, LET IT HEAL, AND LET IT GO.
—*@RealTalkKim*

That kind of total transformation is possible, and it's a decision away. Are you ready to make that decision? If so, I challenge you to inventory your heart and get busy releasing anything that might have you stuck. It is really that simple, and the decision is yours!

Heavenly Father, I thank You for the choices that I get to make every day. I consider them a gift. Thank You for the understanding and wisdom that You are releasing into my life. Give me the courage to get real with myself and deal with the hard things that keep me hung up in seasons I need to put behind me. I am free in Jesus' name. Amen!

I DECLARE

I decree and declare breakthrough in every area of my life. No weapon formed against me shall prosper. I release the negatives and embrace the blessings.

CHAPTER 4

MOVE FORWARD

SOMETIMES LIFE PARALYZES you and prevents your next step. The tragedy is that when you shrink from moving forward, you set yourself up to fear change and accept stagnation. Do you know people who avoid change and allow challenges to put them in a box? They feel safe and content as long as everything stays the same. They feel threatened when anything changes. Then they wonder why life seems to pass them by.

I can tell you that this is not what God intended. If the Creator of the universe could breathe life into us and speak the world into existence, don't you think He wants greater things for us than we could even imagine?

Of course He does! Yet if the enemy can keep us bound by fear, he will successfully steal our purpose. How else can he oppose God and destroy the deliverer in each of us?

At the same time, we oppose ourselves. When life doesn't go according to our plans, we see it as a signal to hit the brakes, which is how paralysis begins. But does that make any sense? Do you know anyone who has never experienced pain? I don't. Everyone has suffered loss, whether it involves marriage, finances, jobs, children, or health. So should everyone quit moving forward?

Face it: pain touches us all. How you deal with pain makes all the difference. You can become intentional, overcome your trauma, and refuse to be robbed of life's pleasures. Or you can settle for just existing from day to day—going to work, making dinner, watching TV, and going to bed. You can live that kind of life in your sleep because you are not *present*. You no longer think about the joys of life. You don't notice the flowers blooming or children laughing. Gone is the anticipation of anniversary dinners, career promotions, and graduations. You don't allow yourself to hope because you think all hope is lost.

Emotional paralysis occurs for many reasons. You might learn to tolerate your pain rather than deal with its root causes. This leaves you numb to those you should be calling to account—those who create havoc in your life. Maybe your own decisions have triggered your current circumstances, and you bury your pain by "just living with" whatever befalls you.

PAIN TOUCHES US ALL.
HOW YOU DEAL WITH PAIN MAKES ALL THE DIFFERENCE.
—*@RealTalkKim*

There is a better way. Even if you do not know the way out of your troubles, you can walk in forgiveness and repent of the choices that have caused you pain. In this chapter you will find biblical and personal examples of how to take up your bed of affliction and walk.

STORMS, SEASONS, AND SYMPTOMS OF UNTREATED PAIN

As long as blood is running through your veins, you will have bad days and tough seasons. Storms will come and wreak havoc in your life. You might even go from one storm to another and wonder why. The good news is that every storm runs out of rain sometime. Your storm is at most a season, not a life sentence. That does not mean hellacious storms won't sometimes pile on. You don't just lose your job;

the car breaks down too. You don't just get divorced; your doctor finds a tumor at the same time.

This is what I meant when I said that Satan can't take you out, so he'll try to wear you out. When that happens, you must step back and take stock. Ask yourself questions such as, "How did I get here, and why? Did I refuse to see what was on the horizon? What changes must I make?"

This is also the time to welcome God into your situation. Ask Him to show you where you need to make adjustments so you can break generational curses and other negative patterns. I have already said that generational curses are real, but when you receive Christ into your heart, He lives inside you. So the same power that raised Jesus from the dead lives in you and will set you free from bondages that try to imprison you.

But you cannot be healed of the pain you ignore. You have to deal with whatever has devastated you. Hiding behind a mask and a fake smile will not ward off your restless nights. If you want to be free, honesty is the best policy.

Every day I correspond with people who are stuck and unable to move forward. They cannot figure out how to exit one season and enter another, so they let things ride and those circumstances define their entire lifetimes. This happens because they are not being honest, not even with themselves. Until they face what imprisons them and admit what they have allowed, they will have more of the same.

Often the things you tell yourself cause your greatest heartaches. Without realizing it, you can treat what you say as a binding commitment. I'm talking about pronouncements such as "I'll never love again" or "I'll never break free of that person's influence over my life." You choose whether to make those statements, but you can also choose to renounce them.

Recognize your untreated pain, and recognize your strength, which comes from the Lord. He said that He would never leave nor forsake you. (See Hebrews 13:5.) He does not walk away from you. He is with you no matter how lonely you feel. Don't allow your past denial of your pain to negate your relationship with Jesus Christ. That relationship cannot be measured against your earthly relationships. We are broken vessels, and we will continue to fail. However, failure is not defeat until you quit trying. Decide to leave negativity and illicit relationships behind you. Determine that you will no longer admit unwelcome intruders into your life to hijack your faith and rob you of your peace. It is time for your pain to be healed.

> ### IF YOU'RE NOT WILLING TO CHANGE, DON'T EXPECT YOUR LIFE TO EITHER!
> —@RealTalkKim

REVEAL YOUR PAIN

You cannot heal what you are not willing to reveal, especially when shame keeps you hiding. Shame over what happened to you can keep you bound to your pain. However, when you are ready to walk free, you will no longer allow shame to keep you from revealing your past.

For many years I did not mention my first marriage. When I wrote my first book, I sensed God saying that I had to talk about it. He and I went back and forth on this because to me it was as though it never happened. Yet it did happen, and it was part of my past. My revealing that aspect of my life was part of my healing walk. I realized that in order to love people back to life, I needed to be honest with them and with myself.

What happened to you is not just about you but about all those beautiful people who need someone to speak up and bare all. People tell me every day that they are looking for a pastor who has survived being broken. They want someone who has received a message from their mess—someone like Jabez.

> Now Jabez was more honorable than his brothers,
> and his mother called his name Jabez, saying,
> "Because I bore him in pain." And Jabez called on
> the God of Israel saying, "Oh, that You would bless
> me indeed, and enlarge my territory, that Your
> hand would be with me, and that You would keep
> me from evil, that I may not cause pain!" So God
> granted him what he requested.
>
> —1 Chronicles 4:9–10

The prayer of Jabez was significant in my restoration process. His name suggests pain and sorrow.[1] We know that biblical names were given for more than identification. They are descriptive of the names' bearers. Can you imagine growing up with a name everyone knew was connected to pain? The mother of Jabez marked him for long-term misery, having named him because of her own suffering. Nonetheless, he was called honorable by God.

As I studied this prayer, I saw that the word *honorable* used in this text refers to glory.[2] I believe the glory of God was upon the pain and sorrow of Jabez. His story is a great illustration as we choose to make life changes. Scripture reveals his prayer, which remains a pattern even today.

Notice that Jabez prayed for God to do five things: (1) bless him, (2) enlarge his territory, (3) keep His hand upon him, (4) keep him from evil, and (5) keep him from causing others pain. Let's explore his requests in relation to our lives.

Bless me indeed.

Jabez prayed *despite* his suffering. He had done nothing to deserve the name he was given. Most of us would say we don't deserve the humiliation and pain that has been inflicted on us.

I believe one exception is the case of Isaac's son Jacob. His name suggests that he was a supplanter or trickster, which he was. He even tricked his father into giving him the family birthright instead of giving it to the rightful heir, his twin brother, Esau. Unlike Jabez, Jacob thought life was all about him. I believe God was sick of his deceiving ways. So he had a "wrestling match" with him at Peniel. Stubborn Jacob wrestled all night and would not let God go until He blessed Jacob, whose name was then changed to Israel, which means "God prevails."[3]

Jacob said he came face to face with God, who spared his life, left him with a lifetime limp, and gave him a new name. Wrestling with God introduced Jacob to himself. Although Jacob was different from Jabez, both men contended for their identities and callings. There was a definite sign of change in Jacob's life because he refused to give up.

It's time for you to have a one-on-one discussion with God about who you are becoming and who He has called you to be. Like Jabez and Jacob, it doesn't matter who you were before your encounter with God. You need only perseverance and a change of heart to be blessed. One decision changes everything.

As it was with these men, the injury I experienced sparked change not only in my life but also in thousands of other lives. I could not have written my story as it is today. I had to face the fear of my future without my marriage, my business, my home, and even my husband. The choice I made to release all unforgiveness, bitterness, and anger helped create the platform I have today. It was my own Peniel. I began desiring time alone in the presence of God. No one could give me the satisfaction God did as I allowed Him to heal me from within. Like Jacob, I had to wrestle with my will and His will for my life.

You too have a call from God to do great things. The enemy will do everything possible to distract and destroy you before you step into your purpose. It is up to you to move from where you are to where you are destined to be.

YOUR DESTINY ISN'T GOING ANYWHERE WITHOUT YOU.
—*@RealTalkKim*

Enlarge my territory.

As my parents, my boys, and I traveled through the gates of my upscale community with all my possessions in tow, I knew I was leaving a life built on pretense. My husband and I had a fabulous home, luxury cars, and designer clothes. Yet we had drifted from our first love, and Jesus Christ was no longer our mainstay. The friends I entertained were no longer there for me. The success I once craved no longer filled the void that enveloped my entire family. My little boys did not deserve what their parents were putting them through. They lost family, home, and friends and had no idea what their tomorrow would look like.

I knew my life had to change drastically. I had to break out of the box my expectations created and allow God to work something unlike anything I had ever imagined. What I discovered is that God never fails to deliver an upgrade. The life I have now cannot compare with what I lost. He has enlarged my territory above and beyond what I could have envisioned. My life is full of new adventures and exciting experiences.

Let Your hand be with me.

The hand of God is synonymous with the protection and provision of God. Many of the storms and injuries in my life were created by my choices. Some happened when I was placed in detrimental situations by other people's actions. I had to survive the divorce and the chaos that surrounded my life at that time. God's divine protection kept me from dangers seen and unseen. Based upon what I know He protected me from, I can only imagine what the unseen dangers were.

God's hand was on my life. His hand is on your life too. You can have the assurance that God is your protection and provision, if you will allow Him to be. Even when you cannot see your way out, you can still decide that you are ready for change. One step forward is all it takes.

Keep me from evil.

During my healing process I remember wishing that my ex would be hit by a train. I would pray, "Don't kill him, Lord. Just hurt him really bad." I was speaking out of hurt, anger, and bitterness. You see, hurt people hurt people, and healed people heal people. When I was hurting, I was in no position to help anyone. As soon as I allowed God to do a good work within me, my perception and attitude changed. I realized that my marriage had given me two of the greatest gifts in my life: my boys.

> ## GOD MAY NOT RESTORE IT BECAUSE HE'S GOING TO REPLACE IT WITH SOMETHING BETTER!
> —*@RealTalkKim*

Because of what He taught me, I will always be grateful to God for allowing me to walk through that painful season and also for bringing me out healed and whole. Now I can help so many people who are in the same or similar situations.

The enemy likes to attack the area in which you have found victory. To keep from doing evil, you must speak life over your mind, renewing it with His Word. That takes a continual and daily walk with Christ. Learn to take authority over your thoughts. It is easy to seek revenge. It even seems justifiable at times. But why risk your great purpose and destiny for the sake of getting even? Stop trying to retaliate against those who dropped or labeled you.

Change always comes from within. I can remember the Lord speaking to me one night in my brokenness and saying, "Kimberly, live in such a way that people will see a totally new person." Now people from my past seek me out on social media and in ministry meetings to heap love and blessings on me. They can't see the old Kimberly any longer.

When I moved forward, I was like a small lizard I saw shedding its skin one Easter Sunday morning. It was perched on a frond of my parents' palm tree, and with each step it left bits of skin behind. I began thinking that even that little lizard was being dressed for Resurrection Sunday.

I have not arrived. I am still a work in progress. That is why I understand your challenges and your pain—and why I know you can be made whole.

Help me not to cause pain.

As we walk out the coming action chapters, it will be important to decide not to be the cause of other people's pain. Jabez's prayer is so significant in part because it acknowledges that our lives affect others.

My divorce injured me, but it also affected my sons, who needed their mama to recover. When my family of three moved in with my parents, they were pastoring and had just downsized their home. As I settled into my new life, I grieved over everything I had lost. It was all about me. I could not get past the reality that I was totally dependent on my parents again.

Imagine that—the rebellious child who left home at eighteen because she wanted her independence was far from independent eighteen years later. I was in my parents' home with my two little boys, who were full of anger and missing their daddy. They had done nothing to deserve the loneliness and humiliation of starting over. I knew I had to get up each morning and become the mother they needed me to be. I did not want to be depressed, sad, and broken, but when my healing process was just beginning, I didn't know how *not* to be those things.

Besides my kids needing me healed, I needed myself healed. I am thankful that my parents gave me the opportunity to lead worship at the church. At the time, I felt forced into something I wasn't ready to handle. However, my dad knew I would find peace as I sang again. Leading worship was how God allowed my gift to make room for me. It was preparation for an even greater platform and ministry. Singing was the one thing I knew I was good at. God also brought a childhood desire back to mind: I had wanted to preach, but our denomination restricted women from doing so.

Now, Sunday after Sunday, I stood on the platform singing and leading people into worship. On the inside I was an emotional firepit. My parents knew about my private struggles but allowed me to sing and lead worship anyway. They covered me in prayer and covered for me when I was in despair. One Saturday night I came home drunk after a long night of partying. After I stumbled my way into bed, my daddy entered my room and waited for me to recognize his presence in the darkness before he spoke.

Realizing that he would not leave until I turned toward him, I opened my eyes and saw a man who loved me unconditionally, the way God loved me. He didn't preach to me or condemn me. Instead, he gently said, "I hope you don't have a hangover in the morning, baby girl, because you are still leading worship. You are going to praise your way through."

I looked into the very eyes of mercy. The shame I felt within myself was enough for me to decide never to do that again. It was the first time I felt conviction and took responsibility for myself and my decisions.

It would be easy to say that I did everything right after that. But I'm Real Talk Kim, so let's keep it real. I continued to mess up and did not always do the right thing. My heart was still broken, and I did not know how to put it back together. I had always been able to fix my problems with temporary solutions, but none of that was working anymore.

Now I had to face my problems head-on. The reality of

my life and its imperfections overwhelmed me. First I saw myself for everything I was not and some things I did not want to be, such as a messed-up, twice-divorced woman. Then I saw myself as God saw me—as a woman He created in His image and likeness. I called myself *pitiful*, but He called me *powerful*. I decided right then that I had to move forward, bless others, and cause no one pain.

> **GOD DOESN'T LOVE SOME FUTURE, GOT-IT-ALL-TOGETHER VERSION OF YOU. HE LOVES YOU RIGHT NOW, EVEN IN YOUR MESS!**
> —*@RealTalkKim*

As you forgive yourself and receive God's forgiveness, understand that you will fall sometimes. God never quits loving you because you make poor decisions. He helps you decide to get up one more time.

DESPERATE FOR BREAKTHROUGH

I talked earlier about the Samaritan woman who met Jesus when He stopped at the well in Sychar. (See John 4.) She was amazed that Jesus asked her for a drink, and she questioned His intentions. In those days Jewish men did not even speak to Samaritan women. Yet Jesus did. He told her about living water and about her five husbands and the man she was now living with.

The woman realized that Jesus was no ordinary man. When He said she could receive a fountain of water springing up into everlasting life, she wanted it! She left her water pot and ran into the city, inviting everyone to come and see this man who knew her life story. Because she moved forward and allowed the Lord's presence to change her from the inside out, a Samaritan revival happened. Everyone saw the change in her and wanted it for themselves.

God doesn't always work on our timetable, but He does work with us when we get real with ourselves. In a single moment God can change your entire life. When you choose to get back up even though everything within you wants to stay down, you walk in victory. Everyone in your world, including your loved ones, will give you permission to roll over and die in your misery. Yet you can decide to make it through another day.

Only God knows why you are still breathing. He knows your history of just existing. He knows you faced another failure but decided to get up anyway. The deliverer inside you won't let you stay down. You are built with God stuff, with His breakthrough anointing. The enemy keeps sending distractions to prevent the person you will become on the other side of your trouble. You just need to fix your eyes on the breakthrough. You are not there yet, but you will be!

The Bible says God's Word is a lamp to your feet and a light to your path. (See Psalm 119:105.) It doesn't say that God shines a spotlight for you. No! You must do your part. You must stir up some faith, even hijack somebody else's, if you must. Some people disagree with that idea, but during my divorce, as I led others into worship, I was so low and so desperate for freedom that I would do anything to get it. So I focused on the most active, worshipful lady at church and sat as close to her as I could. I wanted to hijack some of her peace and freedom.

What am I saying? You have to assist in your own breakthrough.

It starts with identifying the lies you tell yourself every day. Fear was a spirit I dealt with often—fear of the unknown, fear of tomorrow, fear of being alone. *Fear.* When God talked with me about my inner brokenness, He walked me through the process of releasing it. Why did it take until I was thirty-six years old? Probably because I wasn't ready before that. I had only known God on the level my parents had taught me. I had never hit rock bottom and never needed Him as desperately as I did in that place. Now there was no way around it. I had to be transparent with myself, face my mistakes, and quit blaming everyone else.

One night while lying in bed, seething with hatred toward the counterfeit people in my world, I screamed out to God to "kill" them.

God just said, "Until you can forgive them, I can't help you."

I bargained with Him and reminded Him of how they treated me. What I found so interesting was His refusal to say even one word about them. He only pointed out my need for healing and forgiveness.

That night my soul turned. With all the hurt, unforgiveness, bitterness, and anger inside me, I released myself to Him and asked Him to come into my heart. I thought I had done that when I was six years old, but I really hadn't. If I had, I would not have been so full of hate and anger thirty years later.

Like never before, I began communicating with God, allowing my heart to speak instead of my flesh. Like Jacob, I said, "God, I'm not leaving this room until You heal me—all of me, every ugly part of me. You have eight hours to do it. My sons are going to need breakfast in the morning, and they need a healed mama to show up."

When I tell you that God came into that room and set me totally free, I mean it. It was as though I became brand-new! My anger left. My brokenness became my healing. I was a woman on a mission, ready to take on a new chapter. I opened my mouth and decreed a new thing over myself. I allowed my heart to be transformed into what God desired it to be.

As one of my close friends says, "It's not about *becoming something* but about *unbecoming* who you became to get people who weren't supposed to be in your life to love you."

THERE'S A BLESSING IN THE BREAKING.
—@RealTalkKim

As you move forward on your journey of freedom, release everyone you have allowed to imprison you with his or her influence, judgments, and counterfeit successes. God created you to live in your lane, which is unlike anyone else's. You cannot stay in your lane and live in comparison. You lose your purpose when you measure your gifts and talents against other people's. Just admit that you have lived too long in shame over what you have allowed, and invite Jesus Christ into your life as your Savior. He is ready to do His part, opening doors that no one can shut!

In the next section we are going to look more closely at some of the obstacles that keep us from walking in freedom and destiny. Before we move forward, thank God for having His hand on your life, and declare His promises over your future. Get ready—God is going to exceed your expectations!

Father, thank You for Your hand of grace in my life. Thank You for knowing the beginning and the end. Your plans for my life are good and not evil. I embrace Your blessings today as I begin to move forward into the abundance You have for me. In Jesus' name, amen.

I DECLARE

I decree and declare that this is a new day and a new week full of favor for me. The right doors are opening, and the wrong ones are closing.

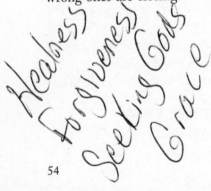

PART II

CONQUERING THE OBSTACLES

God is about to turn your private prayers into public miracles.

CHAPTER 5

SHUT HELL UP

YOU COMMUNICATE WITH people every day, but you probably don't think about the continual dialogue going on in your mind. You may have heard that human beings think tens of thousands of thoughts per day. Whatever the number, you need to distinguish between thoughts that are positive and those that are negative. Both kinds determine your actions.

I can tell you that I have a very active mind, and I have to bring it into subjection to the Spirit of God continually. On a trip to Nigeria I ministered to a dynamic congregation that is setting the spiritual flow for many churches in other countries. From the moment my assistant confirmed the trip, I became both nervous and excited about this amazing opportunity. Not only was it my first international trip, but I would be ministering at an international megachurch.

My parents have traveled all over the world preaching. Now I was continuing that legacy. My dad spoke often of Nigeria and was ecstatic to hear that I would be preaching there. Immediately I thought, "I cannot let my parents down." I wanted to show them I was ready for international travel. The moment I boarded the plane, self-defeating, self-focused thoughts flooded my mind. It was a twenty-hour flight, so my anxiety levels were excruciating.

On the first night I was to preach, I was extremely nervous.

My inner dialogue caused intense agitation, and I thought of every negative thing that could happen. How would the congregation understand my Southern accent? What if because of my ignorance of their culture I said something offensive? What made me think I was ready for this type of ministry anyway?

I was self-focused and forgot that I would not be ministering in my own power anyway. I would have to preach by the power of God within me. That meant taking my thoughts captive and renewing my mind. I knew that I had spent time in the presence of the Lord and had prepared myself for this moment, so I walked onto the platform and allowed the Holy Spirit to use me. God had opened this door. My job was to allow Him to flow through me.

When I came off the platform, however, fearful doubts flooded right back. I worried that the language barrier had made it difficult for people to receive certain things I said. My self-defeating babble wanted to run rampant: "What a stupid thing to say! They didn't hear a word of it! That was the worst message you have ever preached!"

Obviously having an international platform does not necessarily create the feeling that you have arrived. Immediately after the service the pastoral team thanked me for the message and showed such appreciation and honor that I humbly thanked the Lord for using me to accomplish His will. However, on the second night I battled those voices again, until I decided that I would not allow the confusion to determine the outcome.

Thousands of people had returned to hear the word that the Lord had given to me. I preached from my heart and asked Him to anoint it. When I went back to my seat, I knew that I had done my best. I had cast down all imaginations, self-defeating babble, and self-focused thoughts. It wasn't up to me to prove how great God is in my life. All I had to do was speak what He gave me without doubting and let Him fill the hungry hearts before me.

He did! That night I watched God touch big, strong Nigerian men, who had tears flowing down their faces.

It would be untrue to say that I never doubted again. When I left Nigeria, I returned to the States to preach on the same platform as someone I had always admired. I wondered how I could follow in this person's footsteps. What could I say that had not already been said? How could I possibly satisfy the expectations of the people?

Once again, I realized how negative thinking adversely affects our freedom in God. What counts is not how great I am but how great God is. He does not call me to be great anyway; He only wants me to let Him flow through me.

I can tell you that life gets easier when you know that people's expectations are not your concern. Often I wonder why God appointed me to do what I do. I am most satisfied delivering His Word and loving His people, but it did not happen by accident. God chose me to walk out this journey. He called me to travel the world and minister to those who have been broken by people, the past, and fears that control them in the present.

My favorite scripture is Jeremiah 29:11. It says that God knows the plans He has for us—plans to give us hope and a future. Because of our past experiences many of us don't expect that future to unfold. The enemy wants to keep us ashamed and stuck in the past. The bondage is real, but it is in the mind. Salvation is real too. It is a free gift reserved for us by God. But we cannot experience the complete freedom Jesus purchased for us if our minds remain bound. It is up to us to reject the chains of our past mistakes and of the people in our history.

Every day, I encounter people who are bound by the past. They are what I call *free hostages*. They are comfortable in the "convenience" of their bondage. If they stay there, other people will pity them, and they can avoid being accountable for their actions.

Does that speak to your situation? Are you ready to be truly free? Then keep reading! When you get free in your mind, God will clean up everything else.

Stop Judging yourself

SOME BLESSINGS ARE BLOCKED BY WHAT YOU REFUSE TO LEAVE.
—*@RealTalkKim*

Most of my friends can tell you that I frequently lay my hands on my head and tell my thoughts to line up with the Word of God. One night while I was flying home after a powerful week of ministry in multiple cities, the Lord dropped this statement in my spirit: "Shut hell up!" I had been talking to myself and judging every word of my messages, even second-guessing my choice of sermons and wondering what I could have done to be "more anointed."

In His quiet voice God gave me the sweet peace that only He can give and assured me that He was well pleased. It reminded me that I had to stop listening to voices that create hell in my emotions. If I didn't, those voices would govern my actions. It wasn't as though I hadn't already learned that lesson. I knew that I would become what I think about most. I just needed a good, strong reminder.

THE PRESENCE OF CHRIST AND THE RENEWED MIND

The fourth chapter of Philippians has always helped me in times of confusion. It is so powerful because Paul wrote it when he was locked up and in shackles. Like any human being, he might easily have questioned his circumstances and wondered why God allowed them. He could have asked what he had done to deserve such treatment. He might have mentioned being fearful of what was next.

Yet instead of discovering Paul's questions and fears, we

find a man secure enough in his faith to show us how to maintain peace in the midst of our struggles. In the following passage he explains how we shatter the prison of the mind by the way we process our thoughts.

Peace *Family* *Money* *Love* *Job* *Car*

> Don't worry about anything; instead, pray about everything. Tell God what you need, and thank him for all he has done. Then you will experience God's peace, which exceeds anything we can understand. His peace will guard your hearts and minds as you live in Christ Jesus. And now, dear brothers and sisters, one final thing. Fix your thoughts on what is true, and honorable, and right, and pure, and lovely, and admirable. Think about things that are excellent and worthy of praise.
> —PHILIPPIANS 4:6–8, NLT

Your circumstances might be as far from peaceful as Paul's were. Is your marriage in jeopardy? Is your house in foreclosure? Are you in prison? There is hope anyhow! Paul's message is clear: our peace cannot depend upon our circumstances. This life will never be completely free of conflict.

Philippians 4:6 is difficult to accept. Paul tells us not to worry about *anything* but instead to pray about *everything*. That is not always what we want to hear. Yet Paul's words are direct: he tells us that *nothing* should worry us, even the worst possible circumstances.

So why do we allow our inner conversations to drive our stress and control our emotions? Paul said we don't have to. A paradigm shift happens when we understand that changing our thoughts changes our environment and view of God. We were not created to worry. Doing so costs more than we want to pay. Stress creates physical and emotional problems, coupled with spiritual unrest and all kinds of confusion.

So what delivers us from our mess? We can have peace of mind through the mind of Christ. That is how you get free from the anxiety caused by inner voices.

You *can* become a focused person. You can face difficulty without negative self-talk. When you are battling for your mind, get in the Word of God and let it saturate your spirit. Many people ask me how to do that. I say, "Pick your method." There are lots of Bible apps for your cell phone. They make it easy to have the Word with you continuously. Some apps will even read the Word to you as you go to sleep. (If you have trouble falling asleep, just read the Word. The enemy won't want you to stay awake!)

If you are a new believer and have no idea where to begin in the Bible, read a chapter in the Book of Proverbs each day. You can also walk through the Gospels in the New Testament and read about how ordinary people became apostles who did extraordinary things for the kingdom of God. They were simple people like us, called by God to do His work.

LISTEN TO HEAVEN

When worry calls your name, remember that prayer changes things. It will lift you from your depths of despair. In the middle of your crisis, focus on whatever is true, honorable, right, pure, lovely, and admirable, as Philippians 4:8 commands. That will help you partake of the mind of Christ, which brings peace.

Paul did more than explain how peace overcomes our inner confusion; his life demonstrated what he believed. Hearing about peace is one thing, but obeying God's Word—that is where peace becomes real. So pray about everything, as Paul commanded. You cannot go to God in prayer without seeing an outward demonstration of His power. Pray expectantly, knowing that every good and perfect gift comes from Him. (See James 1:17.)

I realized in Nigeria that even when my mind wavered, I could intentionally think about good things. I remembered that I'm not called to be perfect but to be an instrument that God can use. Despite my imperfections, He will shine brighter through me than I could ever shine in my own glory.

Whatever happens, we shut hell up by listening to heaven. Our earthly hell consists of thoughts that keep us broken because we habitually meditate on them—thoughts such as, "I'll never find another great job," "How can I ever trust another man after my husband left me?" or "There's no way I will be able to buy another house after bankruptcy."

GOD HAS A REASON FOR YOUR SEASON.
—*@RealTalkKim*

Those inner voices speak as long as we allow them. The rain falls on the just and the unjust. (See Matthew 5:45.) All of us go through some kind of hardship. Certain seasons drive us toward depression. Others lead us toward anger or bitterness. However, Paul's life proves that we can reject these outcomes. The peace he experienced while in shackles shows us that breaking out is *always* possible.

When you realize that your season has a reason, you can decide that your pain will not be wasted. When you do that, victory is yours! You might take a licking, but you will keep on ticking. Yes, those inner voices might try to drive you to destruction, but you are the one in control.

At my lowest point I prayed and spoke truth to my situation. I said, "Devil, you might have me down for a minute, but I'm getting up and taking other victims with me. They will be victorious as we arise together."

Lots of God's servants get kicked down for a season. Take the great prophet and miracle worker Elijah. His example is powerful! When King Ahab told his wife, Queen Jezebel, that Elijah had killed all the prophets of Baal, Jezebel sent this message to Elijah: "May the gods strike me and even kill me if by this time tomorrow I have not killed you just as you killed them" (1 Kings 19:2, NLT).

Elijah's reaction to the threat was very human:

> Elijah was afraid and fled for his life. He went to Beersheba, a town in Judah, and he left his servant there. Then he went on alone into the wilderness, traveling all day. He sat down under a solitary broom tree and prayed that he might die. "I have had enough, LORD," he said. "Take my life, for I am no better than my ancestors who have already died." Then he lay down and slept under the broom tree. But as he was sleeping, an angel touched him and told him, "Get up and eat!"
>
> —1 KINGS 19:3–5, NLT

In 1 Kings chapter 18 Elijah slew 450 prophets of Baal and 400 prophets of the Canaanite goddess Asherah. Even after this massive success, Elijah fled in fear.

Have you ever faltered after your mountaintop experience? Has fear gripped your heart after a great victory? I know I've been there!

Fear so overtook Elijah that he wanted to die! His prayer was filled with despair but totally honest. God gave His man some correction but also sent help. It just shows that even God's anointed prophets sometimes allow their thoughts to rule. Yet God is with them.

A battle will always be underway in your mind. Knowing this empowers you to become proactive in that battle. If you are a child of God, you know the One in whom you have believed. (See 2 Timothy 1:12.) You know that He never created a nobody. You also know that He created everyone special in her own way.

That includes you. So how many times have you fled the scene of your struggle? Have you run from your bad credit or a bitter disappointment? Has God moved someone out of your life? Are you still allowing that person to control your emotions? Instead of seeing the rejection as God's protection, are you stalking the person on social media and allowing him to hurt you again and again? Online everyone is a click away. If you play that game, the enemy will make sure you read posts from everyone who ever hurt you. Even if you no longer hang out with the people, you will keep "fellowshipping" with them!

> **DO YOURSELF A FAVOR, AND DON'T STAY UPDATED WITH THOSE YOU'VE REALIZED AREN'T GOOD FOR YOU. YOU DON'T NEED TO KNOW WHAT THEY'RE DOING!**
> —*@RealTalkKim*

What you might not realize is that the devil cannot hurt God. Instead, he does whatever it takes to hurt God's people. The enemy's mission is clear: he will keep you bound any way possible. Yet you are not his victim. You can pray!

ESTABLISH A PRAYER LIFE

You might be reading this chapter and saying, "Kim, I'm under my broom tree, and I feel stuck." Wherever I preach, I ask how many people feel stuck. The response is always overwhelming. Most people feel unable to get out of at least one situation.

When I ask the "stuck" question, people expect a profound answer from me. I simply tell them, "Get up and change your situation." I know what they are thinking: "It's not that easy, Kim."

The fact remains that you are just one step away from freedom. To become a strong man or woman who rises up against all odds, you must know who you are in Christ and follow the example of Jesus. He walked in the shoes of a man but performed miracles, healed the sick, and raised the dead. He wasn't able to do this simply because He was God in the flesh. Even Jesus drew Himself away to be alone with God. He was the prime example of prayer, withdrawing from the crowds and nourishing Himself in daily communion with the Father.

If Jesus had to pull away to pray, how much do we need to do the same?

Prayer is the path to freedom! Each day, I wake up knowing that I must focus on my purpose by spending time with the Lord and allowing Him to refresh me. The mighty king and psalmist David did that. He asked the Lord to satisfy him early with His mercy so he could rejoice and be glad. (See Psalm 90:14.) David went through times of depression, just as I do. So he turned to God. The weapons needed to combat depression are not carnal. They are mighty for pulling down *every* stronghold. (See 2 Corinthians 10:4–5.)

God has given me a mandate to illuminate His promises and help you get free from your enemy. When the devil harasses you, rejoice! Thieves are not interested in robbing empty vaults. If the devil did not see gifts and purposes in your future, he would leave you alone. So pray your way out of your pit, and watch God be God in your life.

After returning to my parents' home following my divorce, I could have stayed broken and let my parents raise my boys. But I remember the day my brother walked into my bedroom and ordered me to get up, shower, and find a job. He let me know that changing my life was my decision to make. I never dreamed it would be so easy once I shifted my thinking. If I had known, I would have done it much sooner!

IF THE DEVIL DID NOT SEE GIFTS AND PURPOSES IN YOUR FUTURE, HE WOULD LEAVE YOU ALONE.
—*@RealTalkKim*

Every week, I see people who come to church depressed and miserable, wondering why God has not changed their situations. But it is their choice to make. None of us will ever know the good things God has in store until we take a step toward Him. We can trust Him! He has equipped us to come out of our present situations and make positive life changes.

It is up to us!

SPEND TIME IN WORSHIP

At times I have experienced a mental oppression that seemed almost physical, bringing feelings of heaviness and self-defeating thoughts. I recognized that I was engaged in some sort of spiritual battle but could not immediately free myself. So I prayed. I confessed Scripture. I read God's Word. I prayed some more. Then I entered into worship, which opened me up to change.

Like you, I was born to be a worshipper. There is no one living who should not be worshipping the Creator of the universe. It's not because He needs our worship but because worshipping Him changes us. It changes the way we see God, ourselves, and our circumstances. No matter how insecure, bitter, angry, or unhappy you might be, when you sing songs of praise and worship, instead of focusing on yourself, your attention shifts to the power of the Most High.

Singing isn't the only form of worship. Just waking up

thankful to be alive one more day is an awesome form of worship. Being conscious of God's blessings in your personal life gives you strength to face the trials that come. In worship you defeat them because you come to rely on His power instead of your own.

When my mind becomes encumbered with troubles, I renew it by giving thanks and releasing negative, hindering thoughts. That is when I sense the peace that I have learned to welcome. It doesn't come because my thoughts are positive enough or I am talking myself into or out of something. That might help me temporarily, but it cannot root out the real problem.

You know who the enemy is, and you know that only Jesus Christ can defeat him. So when you see the enemy at work, you fight him with prayer, scriptural truth, and worship. The question is whether you discern the ongoing need to train your mind on the things of God. If you do, victory is inevitable. If you don't, the things of this world will consume you. Going with the negative flow is always easier in the short term, but it is carnal and will not help you to stand by faith.

Remember that Paul said to worry about nothing but pray about everything. That is not as easy as it sounds. Focusing your mind on God requires purposeful, intentional steps. Otherwise, your mind will go wherever it wants, which is nowhere good. Even when you are most confident of God's love and care, you have to decide what you will and will not think about. When Paul told us to think only about things that are pure and holy, He was letting us know we must actively decide how to think.

When I sense that my thoughts are racing, I have to consciously think about what I'm thinking about, and I have to feed on the Word of God. You have those times too. So in case you have a difficult time finding scriptures that work for you, let's do it together.

- Second Corinthians 10:3–5 says, "Though we walk in the flesh, we do not war according to the flesh. For the weapons of our warfare are not carnal but mighty in God for pulling down strongholds, casting down arguments and every high thing that exalts itself against the knowledge of God, bringing every thought into captivity to the obedience of Christ."

  You must understand that you are fighting for your mind. You also need to decide that you are a warrior and you will be victorious.

- Romans 12:2 says, "Do not be conformed to this world, but be transformed by the renewing of your mind, that you may prove what is that good and acceptable and perfect will of God."

  You are the one who decides whether you will allow your mind to become overactive or will welcome the peace that surpasses your understanding. (See Philippians 4:8.)

- A scripture I quote throughout the day is 2 Timothy 1:7: "For God has not given us a spirit of fear, but of power and of love and of a sound mind."

  This scripture reminds me of the Lord's power when I feel as though my mind is in confusion. Do not move forward with decisions when you are driven by confusion. Allow peace to be the standard in your life.

- Proverbs 3:5–6 declares, "Trust in the LORD with all your heart, and lean not on your own understanding; in all your ways acknowledge Him, and He shall direct your paths."

   God's Word provides the direction you need to seek and worship Him with your whole heart. Even when you struggle to find your way, His Word assures you that He will direct your path.

You do not have to be intimidated by the enemy. However, you must recognize his ploys. Knowledge is power. It's time for you to stand up and declare that you are ready for change. Then put that change in motion by getting in the Word of God, establishing your daily prayer time, and allowing worship to be a constant in your life.

> *Dear heavenly Father, help me stop complaining and focusing on the negative. Help me keep my eyes on You. Thank You for being my strength and my refuge. Thank You for being my example and teacher. I am so grateful that I have You to guide and protect me every step of the way. Thank You for helping me stay focused on You. I trust You and put my faith in You. In all that I do, may I glorify You. In the wonderful name of Jesus, amen.*

I DECLARE

I decree and declare by faith that I am strong and consistent in my mind, body, and soul. I will not worry or fear. I trust Jesus to supply all my needs, emotionally, physically, and spiritually. I declare that every aspect of my life will yield abundant fruit. In Jesus' name!

CHAPTER 6

OVERCOMING REJECTION

EJECTION IS PAINFUL, regardless of its cause. The pain level varies from situation to situation and from person to person, but we all experience the sting of rejection at some point in our lives. Too often rejection causes people to become bitter, hateful, angry, and unforgiving, but it doesn't have to be that way.

Rejection is a refusal to accept someone or something. That isn't always a bad thing. When you're rejected by Mr. or Ms. Wrong, or you're not hired for a job that God never wanted for you, rejection can be a blessing in disguise. As I often say, sometimes rejection is God's protection.

But this isn't the kind of rejection that keeps people stuck and not walking in their purpose. The rejection that comes when a parent abandons you or a spouse leaves can be so painful it alters the way you see the world. But I want you to know that it is possible to overcome rejection and accept your place in life despite other people's failings.

God created us to have fellowship with Him. During the creation, God set the planets, stars, clouds, land, and sea in their places and established life in the earth. He planned each day purposefully and established His divine order in all that He created. On the sixth day God molded a man from the dust of the earth, breathed His own life into him, and called him Adam. God later caused a sleep to fall over the man and used one of his ribs to form a helpmate for him, who would be named Eve.

Humankind's season in the Garden of Eden was the most perfect and blissful time that ever was. It lasted until Adam and Eve allowed Satan to deceive them. In that moment, when they ate fruit from the forbidden tree, they invited sin into the world and their relationship. Eve realized that she had done wrong and admitted that the serpent deceived her. However, Adam blamed Eve for their betrayal of God.

FLOWERS GROW BACK EVEN AFTER THEY'VE BEEN STEPPED ON.
SO WILL YOU.
—@RealTalkKim

This set up our world's progression to this day. There are no perfect relationships and no perfect marriages, and there is no way to live the perfect life the first couple experienced before the fall.

FALLEN RELATIONSHIPS

Rejection stemming from failed relationships is one of the most common hurts I see. It's amazing how a little white lie can taint a relationship. It happens every day, and no one can predict all of the repercussions. We only know that sin destroys and that we are fallen creatures dependent on the Lord Jesus Christ for salvation and for help in living as pure and holy as possible. Even with the best of intentions, we fail many times. Therefore, we return to the cross again and again in repentance for God to cover our sins by His grace.

Because sin is what promotes dishonesty in relationships, there is no guarantee that your marriage will be what it was on your wedding day. Do you remember your first date? You knew you had just met Mr. or Ms. Right. Butterflies came from out of nowhere. You had endless conversations about nothing. You got excited when the doorbell rang, and you knew your date had arrived. Your wedding day seemed perfect, but your honeymoon didn't last forever.

Through a lifetime of pain I have learned that no matter how perfectly your relationship starts out, you cannot be good enough, pretty enough, or skilled enough to maintain perfect harmony all the time. Sin is in the mix. You and your spouse have faults and failures. The memories you create can fade under the weight of them. Unless you set things right, day by day, you will end up asking, "Why did it have to end this way?"

People begin new relationships with the best intentions. Newlyweds expect to spend a lifetime with one spouse. They want to do everything possible to make that person happy. Days, weeks, months, or years into the relationship, however, flaws show up and failures occur. In a flash the bubble bursts and the fairy tale is over. The partner who had the perfect combination of looks, personality, and talent now seems perfect to everyone but his or her spouse.

Can you relate? Have you wondered, "How did our beautiful dreams fade?" or "Why do I spend night after sleepless night wondering where my spouse is?" or "Why doesn't anyone see my pain? Why is everyone happy but me?"

In times of crisis, people sometimes rationalize and say, "He didn't mean to hit me. He gets angry and loses his temper for a bit, but he always apologizes in the morning." That may be true, but it does not excuse bad behavior. Some abusive spouses, whether because of intoxication or mental illness, don't even remember what they did the night before. That makes it even easier for their spouse to believe they deserve what they got.

Have you imagined that the abuse would not have happened if you had only acted happier when your spouse came home from work? "Obviously," you think, "I did something wrong."

You believe that bad things happen because of what's

wrong with *you*. You can never seem to measure up; therefore, you have no idea that you are not the real issue. Without realizing it, you allow seeds of rejection to become full-blown trees full of nasty fruit—more fruit than any human being can bear.

It was never meant to be this way. Adam and Eve not only destroyed their paradise but also set up their family (and the world) for a lifetime of hurt, pain, and rejection. Can you imagine how they must have felt when what they'd done dawned on them? When they were cast out of the Garden of Eden, they were prevented from even visiting their former garden of beauty and rest. From that point forward they would have to toil for everything they received and Eve would have to bear children with much pain.

Do you suppose they spent their lifetimes wondering what might have been if they had made the right decision? Can you imagine how they felt as they left the garden and saw angels guarding the entrance so they could never enter again?

What might have seemed like one little mistake did *so much* damage.

SIN HAS NO FAVORITES

When you see other people's circumstances and realize how fallen our world is, it can free you from wondering why you can't get it together. Introspection goes away, and you realize that bad things happen in life, even to good people. You're not the only one in pain.

Bad things have been happening to good people since Adam and Eve's sons Cain and Abel became "firsts" in human history. Cain was a farmer, and Abel was a shepherd. Each man brought his sacrifice to God, and He accepted Abel's offering but rejected Cain's. In his jealousy, Cain murdered his brother. God then banished Cain to a life of wandering.

What happened? Abel did not deserve his fate. Imagine how Adam and Eve felt when one son became the first murderer and another became the first victim. The first couple had to live with the guilt of having established the sin pattern for their family. Not only that, but we are living out of that pattern still today. Many people who did nothing to deserve pain and rejection are suffering right now.

Think about it. Thousands of children cry nightly because they have no one to kiss them good night or give them a hug. They did not ask to be born to drug-addicted parents unable to care for themselves, much less raise an addicted baby. And when older brothers and sisters must care for younger siblings while their parents are out partying in crack houses, the older siblings miss out on their own childhoods.

Drugs are not always the issue. Sometimes there is sickness or other causes of poverty in the family. Whatever the issue might be, the children end up feeling betrayed and rejected because they never had the security they needed to enjoy being young.

Life deals many hard blows. No one comes out unscathed. Your loss is not necessarily caused by something you did. Sometimes you suffer loss because life is unfair. Yet when you lose a business, a child, a parent, or even your home, you wonder why God allowed it when you believe He could have prevented it.

My answer when people question their pain and rejection is always the same: God never puts pain, suffering, or loss on anyone. However, He is always there during the hard times. He said He would never leave us or forsake us (Deut. 31:6; Heb. 13:5).

The whole world was set up for pain when the enemy deceived our first parents, Adam and Eve. Adam watched in silence as the enemy lied to his wife. Then Adam took some of the fruit that he knew was off-limits. God had specifically instructed him, telling him not to eat from the tree of the knowledge of good and evil, but he did it anyway.

God said there would be consequences for disobeying His command. Indeed, there were, and they affected everyone, not just the disobedient couple. That is how sin works. It affects everyone. You may have been faithful in your marriage, but if your spouse had an affair, you suffer. When your spouse walks out, some people will say it is better for everyone involved. Yet you know that's not true. From that day forward every member of your family has to live with the fallout from a broken home.

Even if both partners believe that calling it quits is better in the long run, the children might not agree. Did the parents talk it over with the children or just decide without considering them? How many children will end up carrying guilt because they think that if they had been prettier or smarter or better behaved, their parents would have stayed together?

We know that family and home should be a safe haven. However, it is too often the scene of abuse, betrayal, and molestation. When a child is molested by a family member, it can begin a long journey of seeking love in all the wrong places. You might be that child. Your son or daughter might be that child.

Sin sets people up to experience rejection on every level. You might have learned to accept any type of attention, however inappropriate, because you were betrayed by those you thought would protect you. However, giving yourself to someone for illicit intimacy will only set you up for more harm than you ever imagined.

Ultimately the answer is found at the cross.

SELF-INFLICTED PAIN

The greatest damage from rejection can be the self-inflicted pain it fosters. Because our society is so judgmental, we strive to do our best to be accepted by those who matter to us. When it seems impossible to pass their scrutiny, we develop low self-esteem and become overly self-critical. We wonder why we cannot measure up to other people's standards and why we are not as smart as our siblings. We question why we are not as pretty as our friends, and we completely forget that God never made a nobody.

We always hear that God made everyone special, but we never really think that applies to us. We allow rejection to grip us until we live in the fear of failure, fear of the unknown, and fear of being alone. We process thoughts that say, "I will never find that special person who can love me and expect nothing in return. If my parents couldn't love me, how can I expect anyone else to give me the love I desire?"

These questions come up when you compare yourself with others. You convince yourself that when you apply for college or a new job, you will be rejected. After all, everyone is "better" than you, so how could you stand a chance? And if those closest to you never saw your value, how will perfect strangers find any potential in you?

Rejection-based thoughts will try to consume you and keep you barely living. The consequences can drive you to extremes such as overachievement or self-destructive lifestyles in which you expect nothing from anyone.

I am so thankful that God never leaves us in our pain and rejection. He deliberately arranges divine appointments with certain people who say the right words at the right time to pull us out of our rejection-fueled depression. He brings people around us who recognize the abilities or talents that we don't see as being valuable—a beautiful voice, an ability to write, skill in throwing a baseball, or the coordination of a great cheerleader or dancer.

If we allow rejection to rule our lives, the seeds of self-hatred will eventually produce mature trees with many branches. But there is another way.

One of my favorite passages of Scripture is Psalm 139, where David writes about God's perfect knowledge of man. He says that God has searched us and knows everything about us, both in our sitting down and our rising up. There is nothing we will ever say that God does not know ahead of time. There is no place to run from His presence, even if we make our beds in hell.

He knows our pain, and God *will* heal our rejection.

FEARFULLY AND WONDERFULLY MADE

The psalmist reminds us that although some decisions bring hell on earth, God is there. In Psalm 139 David explores the creativity of God as He formed us in our mothers' wombs. He says that we are "fearfully and wonderfully made" (v. 14) and explains that God's thoughts toward us are so innumerable that we are virtually unable to count them (v. 18).

THE DEVIL WANTS YOU TO PAY ATTENTION TO YOUR FEELINGS. JESUS WANTS YOU TO PAY ATTENTION TO HIS TRUTH.
—*@RealTalkKim*

Are you getting my point? When you realize that God loves you beyond your ability to give or experience love, it will break the pain of your rejection and become revelation, which is power. You are not what people have called you. You are not how you feel about yourself. You are who God says you are. You are fearfully and wonderfully made.

When you've been rejected, you can develop a fear of rejection that keeps you in bondage and prevents you from walking in your absolute best. When you realize, however, that you are fearfully and wonderfully made, you can break out and become the amazing person David describes in Psalm 139.

Your strength was never in others. It was always in God. If you are His, He is the strength deep within you. When you truly know this, you become an unstoppable force. You still live in a fallen world. Pain is still inevitable, and those who are closest to you might inflict the most pain. However, you don't have to be destroyed by the rejection you suffer.

You can leave behind the brokenness and rejection that betray your God-given value. How? In Jesus. You have a Savior who deliberately went to the cross of Calvary to take your sins and suffering in His body. He did it so you might become righteous. Therefore, you now live, move, and have your being in Him—*if* you submit your life to His covering. (See Acts 17:28.)

You and I are called to love people. When push comes to shove, we cannot make anyone change. However, we can choose wisely and keep those who continually reject and humiliate us from entering our private worlds. As I always say, "Love them from afar. Move them out of your front row and into the balcony of your life."

In a fallen world you can expect to experience some rejection. Your responsibility is to learn how to handle it in a godly way and move on. Personally, I could only have moved on by the grace of God. I would forgive and then sense the hatred rising inside me again. I learned that forgiveness had to be part of my daily walk. Until I learned to forgive continually, I could not get free from pain and rejection. As memories of rejection resurfaced and tried to pull me back into despair, I began speaking life to my situation.

THERE ARE SOME PEOPLE YOU HAVE TO LOVE FROM AFAR. MOVE THEM OUT OF THE FRONT ROW AND INTO THE BALCONY OF YOUR LIFE.
—*@RealTalkKim*

I now refuse to allow anyone who is no longer in my world to rule my everyday life. Whenever I get negative thoughts, I lay hands on my head and speak life to the situations that are trying to overrun my thinking. Today I understand that the key to releasing the memories of rejection is replacing them with the good thoughts and good people God brings into my life. I cannot change what happened in my past, but I can have a joy-filled life because of the changes I make on the inside. I have the power to move on and become the strong person God fearfully and wonderfully made me to be—and so do you.

> *Father, today I submit to You my past, present, and future. Be Lord of all my decisions, and help me to decide wisely. I forgive everyone who has brought rejection into my life. I release each one to Your grace and mercy. In Jesus' name, amen.*

I DECLARE

I decree and declare that I will never be the same. I choose to be intentional about letting go and being free from pain and rejection. I will not allow anyone to set me up for failure. I am fearfully and wonderfully made, and I know that my heavenly Father continually thinks about me.

CHAPTER 7

STRAIGHT OUTTA EXCUSES

MOST PEOPLE MAKE excuses for why they are not experiencing freedom. Too often they blame others, never taking responsibility for their own actions. Yes, life deals us tough blows sometimes, but that doesn't mean we can wallow in our situations, waiting for someone else to change them.

I once lived a life ruled by excuses. It all started in childhood when I accepted labels people gave me and allowed them to become my name. A learning disability answered why I could not make better grades, go to college, or follow directions from my parents. Honestly I did not really understand what the term *learning disability* meant. Yet it became an albatross around my neck, and I allowed those two words to limit my ability to function *for years*.

You could say I became the victim in my own story. It took me thirty-six years to realize that my story could change and I could alter the trajectory of my life. I could choose to forgive those who had moved me through the educational system without finding an answer for my struggles. I did not have to live with a victim mentality just because people and situations injured me. I could resist the natural tendency to blame others. Blame seemed like a good crutch to lean on, but it only created more pain. So at thirty-six I decided to face my fear and move beyond where I'd been.

Perhaps more than anything else, forgiveness was the key to overcoming my hurts and changing my story. I also learned that what you name your situations has a lot to do with how they turn out. In Genesis 35 Jacob's wife Rachel gave birth to their second son. Realizing her complications during labor would take her life, she named her new baby Ben-Oni, meaning "son of my sorrow"[1] or son of my suffering. After Rachel died, Jacob gave the child the more positive name Benjamin, meaning "son of the right hand"[2] or favorite son.

As Benjamin matured, he could have reverted to the name Ben-Oni, especially because the mother he never had the privilege of knowing had chosen it. However, he chose to remain the right-hand son his father envisioned. Benjamin refused the label that would have defined him through sorrow, even though choosing that name could have permitted him to make excuses about why life was so unfair.

Benjamin's choice would have a lasting impact. The Bible tells us that Saul of Tarsus (who later became the apostle Paul, writer of roughly half of the New Testament) came from the tribe of Benjamin. Rachel's son Benjamin had no idea of the greatness that would be in his lineage, but his powerful decision made a bright future possible for him and his descendants.

OWNING IT

When you face challenges, you can lose sight of the blessings that set up the life you live today. God originally gave me a platform through social media. As I rehearse my humble beginnings in ministry, I realize that God took a life challenge and turned it into my good. I had an hour's drive to work, and each day, the beautiful car that I desperately wanted would overheat and leave me stranded on the interstate. I learned to be patient and let it cool down so I could pour coolant into the radiator, and eventually it would be up and running again.

One day as I looked at the smoke pouring out of my engine, a God idea caused me to pick up my cell phone as I waited for the car to cool down. I thought, "Showtime! If I have to sit along the road with this 'hooptie' every day, I'm going to make it count."

So I started recording myself on my phone: "Hello, awesome people! Are you sitting along the side of the road in a broken-down hooptie wondering how in the world your life has come to this? Remember, Jesus has it all in control!" Within a few days, that video went viral. Thousands of people were commenting about how those few words inspired them to just keep going.

It is comical to think that those videos eventually would lead me to preach to thousands weekly, write books, and appear on television and radio. My ministry was definitely not planned or marketed, yet God has opened thousands of doors for me to minister His Word. And it all started because my car broke down every day.

YOU THINK THE BATTLE IS BIG, BUT WAIT UNTIL YOU SEE THE BLESSING!
—@RealTalkKim

Without a doubt, I never expected to overcome the consequences of my poor decisions. However, my parents had already set the example of serving God despite persecution. I watched them turn their hardships into blessings for others. They continually reminded me that you cannot fight the wrong things people do to you by inflicting more harm. So when I stood in the valley of decision, facing the consequences of all that I had allowed in my life, the choice was clear. To receive the peace that I had never known, I would have to change my actions.

I knew the adage "You reap what you sow," and I seemed to be reaping plenty. I had spent years critiquing other people and blaming them for my hurt and pain. I wondered why my ex-husbands were pictures of perfection until we walked down the aisle and became husband and wife. I did not understand why they never became the protectors I desperately needed.

But when I looked in the mirror and realized that I was half of the equation in my two marriages, I finally quit blaming everyone else. Making excuses wasn't helping my boys, who wept because they had also lost everything. I could not blame everything on their dad. I had to step up and become accountable for my own misjudgments. As much as I suffered, they were suffering too. I knew I had to quit blaming and start forgiving if I ever expected my boys to do the same.

When we leave our mothers' wombs, we come into life as blank slates with no personal faults or failures. We are totally dependent on those who feed and clothe us. If the home is peaceful, we develop a sense of security. If we do not receive the necessary love and affection, we develop feelings of distrust. As we progress into the toddler years, we discover the inborn ability to cry, whine, and even have temper tantrums when we need or desire something. When we learn to talk and find new ways to misbehave, we learn to shift blame. When we are asked whether something unmentionable has happened, we reply, "No," even when it's obvious that we messed up.

We naturally tend to cover up our issues. When my brother and I were in our teens, we were caught red-handed when lying to our mother about an incident. Because my brother was the oldest and was expected to set the better example, my mother asked him why he lied. His answer was remarkable: "Mom, it's just easier to lie than to tell the truth."

As the mother of two sons, I can attest that my boys never stood in line to report the dishonest things they did when I wasn't looking. In fact, when caught, they immediately backtracked and told me why they should not be punished.

Excuses, excuses, excuses!

Making excuses might come naturally to us, but to grow and live abundantly, we have to own our stuff and decide to be straight outta excuses.

STAYING IN YOUR LANE

Because my ministry began on social media, I am continually posting comments and checking the posts of my followers. There are many pros and cons in being connected to the world via social media. One positive effect in the case of Facebook is Timehop. It brings up posts from a year ago and shows what you have accomplished since then. Hopefully it encourages you by showing you how much you have matured over time.

Because my husband and I have only been pastoring for a short time, we realize that we have made many decisions too quickly. I pray often that our church family will bear with our learning process. Recently through Timehop I realized that our worship team had grown exponentially in the past year. I became so excited because, even with our growth pains, I saw that God was in the middle of the process. We didn't grow because we had shaped the team; we had simply allowed God to mold and make it the way He determined it should be.

We can't control every process that takes place in our lives. It's only when we allow God's presence to be present *to us* that change comes. Too many people feel that unless they are in the middle of everything, nothing will be accomplished. That is called *insecurity*. Whether they realize it or not, these people fear that if they do not "shine" through the process, someone else might get the glory. They worry what everyone will think if they are not in the thick of everything.

This is the truth: my husband and I did not know how to lead this growing congregation to where it is today. Yet God has done an abundant work that amazes us. He has talked to me through the process, saying: "Do you see how the teams are working? Even when you are out of town, do you see how many people still come to church?"

My husband and I have realized that we must stay in our lane. *Staying in your lane* has become one of my favorite expressions during these months of growth. God let me know that I could no longer micromanage teams that knew more about a particular thing than I did. God does not need me in their lane. He needs me in my lane.

So often our expectations of the way things "should be" lead us to make bad decisions that end in disappointment. When God first called Moses, one of Israel's greatest leaders, he answered with the words "Here I am." Then as God revealed that He wanted Moses to lead the Hebrews out of Egypt and into the Promised Land, Moses allowed his thoughts to rule him. He looked in the mirror of life and realized he was not brave enough, smart enough, or strong enough to lead two million people out of Egypt.

Did Moses suppose God did not recognize his shortcomings? Was God unaware that Moses had killed an Egyptian? Did He not notice that Moses ran in fear to the Midian desert? Had God not seen him hiding there for forty years? Did He now expect a broken man to rise to the occasion without raising a question or offering an excuse? Absolutely!

We know Moses told God that he was incapable of

speaking for his people. He had a stammer and knew he would struggle to speak before Pharaoh. So God gave him his brother, Aaron, as his spokesperson. God already knew how the journey would end. He knew Moses would become a great leader—the strong leader the Israelites needed. Moses may have committed murder and failed the bravery test. However, God knew he had the fortitude to lead His people out of bondage. So He called Moses into his lane.

FROM "LESS THAN" TO LEADER

Moses was as ordinary as any man or woman. Although he was raised in Pharaoh's palace as the son of Pharaoh's daughter and schooled by the best educators of his day, Moses was called back to his own people. At the age of forty he saw an Egyptian guard beating an Israelite. Moses killed the guard and hid his body, attempting to remove the evidence of his crime. The next day, as he walked among the Israelites, he tried breaking up a fight between two of them. One man remarked, "Do you intend to kill me as you killed the Egyptian?" (Exod. 2:14).

Moses knew he was in trouble and Pharaoh would soon find out what he had done. So he fled into the desert. However, he could not hide from God, who came to where Moses was and called him to lead the Israelites out of bondage.

You can probably understand why Moses gave God excuses as to why he was not the greatest choice to lead God's people. He had failed miserably as an Egyptian prince and heir to Pharaoh. Now he lived quietly in the desert, caring for his father-in-law's flocks. Why would a man who felt so "less than" dare to rock the boat? Why would he, of all people, confront Pharaoh? What made God think the people of Israel would even follow Moses out of Egypt? And how could Moses impress Pharaoh enough to let the children of Israel go?

Excuses, excuses!

God answered each of them until Moses ran out of excuses to give. He realized that God was God and would do as He pleased. That is how it is with God. When He is ready to propel you into your destiny, all the excuses your imagination can muster will not persuade Him to relent.

Moses knew that he could not change God's mind. So when Moses finished rehearsing his excuses, he accepted God's calling to lead the Israelites out of captivity. He did that faithfully for forty years. As Moses' journey unfolds in Scripture, we see a man who once ran from trouble becoming a man who faced every obstacle with faith. Moses never backed down in a crisis. The man with a million reasons not to lead eventually led the people out of bondage and all the way to the precipice of the Promised Land.

WHEN GOD IS READY TO PROPEL YOU INTO YOUR DESTINY, ALL THE EXCUSES YOUR IMAGINATION CAN MUSTER WILL NOT PERSUADE HIM TO RELENT.
—@RealTalkKim

Moses was a mighty warrior, allowing God to work through him to see terrible nations defeated. He fasted for days and spent time alone with God to receive the Ten Commandments. He became a strong leader who watched God provide water and food when there was none to be had. Because he saw God work miracles, he trusted Him to protect Israel against every enemy.

God works with each of us where we are and prepares us for where He determines we will go. Remember that Moses was living in Midian because he ran from danger. Yet God called him to be a great leader, and he ultimately authored the first five books in the Bible. I believe that in being honest with himself about his shortcomings and his uncertainty, Moses released himself to be used by God.

So why should you make excuses when God calls you out of your situations into new places of rest in Him? After a marital or financial failure, it may seem as if you cannot face a new challenge lest you fail again. But is that the truth? After years of being single, why can't you accept a date from a godly man who is well loved by everyone in the church? After leasing for years, why can't you buy a home or a new car? Just because you failed before does not mean you will fail again.

DEAL WITH THE PERSON IN THE MIRROR

You must be honest with yourself. The only way to be free from your fears is to admit that you are allowing them to define your present and limit your future.

Today is the day to tell the man or woman in the mirror, "It's time to move on." If you cannot seem to take the first step, make an appointment with your pastor, a counselor, or a good friend. Be honest with someone you're willing to allow into your private world. Let that person know why you have so many reservations about the decisions you face. Explain why you cannot accept the job promotion you were offered or why you keep rejecting a certain friend who wants to take your relationship to the next level.

Maybe you have disappointed your family or alienated your children. As long as you are breathing, there is hope for healing. Romans 12:2 says not to be conformed to this world but to be transformed by the renewing of your mind so you can prove God's will for your life. Transformation is key because you will never rise above the limitations of your character. There are dozens of examples of celebrities and other high-profile individuals who ended up in the media spotlight because their bright public personas did not match their hidden character.

In a fallen world no one can claim to *never* disappoint or hurt anyone. The only way to approach holy living is to be transformed by Jesus Christ, accept Him as Lord of your life, and allow Him to renew your mind and transform you day by day. Accept your shortcomings and get on with it. Making excuses only creates more self-centeredness. If you cannot accept direction from others without criticizing them, admit that you have an issue that is preventing your growth. If fear has backed you into a corner, face it down.

During my journey of release I realized that self-growth does not just happen. It is the result of persistently seeking God and understanding His plan. Often the gap between who you are and what you can become is filled with unconscious beliefs and outdated habits. You begin to believe everything people say, even when you know it isn't true. Some will build you up by telling you how great you are doing when you know you could do a much better job. These people are not your friends. Friends are honest with you. They will tell you that you need to change, but they will love you through the process. For growth to happen, you need people in your life whom you can trust to speak honestly to you and who will allow you to speak honestly to them.

DON'T LET YOUR FEARS DEFINE YOUR PRESENT
AND LIMIT YOUR FUTURE.
—@RealTalkKim

Jesus lets us know in Matthew 16:24 that we must deny ourselves and take up our cross and follow Him. Denying yourself means focusing on God's interests instead of your personal gratification. We humans tend toward self-centeredness, but not everything is about us. Even other people's opinions are not about us and should not determine our attitude and altitude.

We live in flesh bodies, but as believers in Christ, we have God's Spirit residing in us. This gives us the power to let go of our desires, crucify our flesh, and make decisions that glorify God.

FROM EXCUSE MAKING TO CHANGE MAKING

When asked why they are addicted, many substance abusers use their upbringing to excuse their failures. "My father was an alcoholic" or "My mother was a drug addict" are common excuses for why they can't break their habit. They have convinced themselves there's no use trying.

When my brother and I were in high school, my grandparents moved into our home. My grandfather had been a pastor and had built churches as a young man. My grandmother was always by his side. As I learned about their history, my respect for them increased exponentially, and I gained a greater appreciation for the heritage they passed down to my mother and then to my brother and me.

I was amazed to learn that my grandfather was the first in a family of alcoholics to give his heart to the Lord. Because his dad used the family income to finance his drinking sprees, the family was forced to fish in order to eat. My grandfather and his brothers soon reflected the image of their dad. After marrying my grandmother, my grandfather once came home so sick from a drunken spree that he cried out to her for help. She told him she would not live with a drunk and would never help him clean up after his drunkenness. He would have to decide whether he was going to make a change or be single.

My grandfather decided that he wanted his marriage to work and to be a good father, so he sought help from local pastors. He then began Bible studies and saw his alcoholic brothers and father become solid Christians. My grand-father's conversion changed his family and their community. Two of his brothers also became ministers and pastored for many years.

Back when my grandmother took a stand against her husband's drinking, my grandfather could have blamed his behavior on being raised in a dysfunctional household, where his father abused alcohol. Yet he didn't make excuses. *He chose to change.*

Because of my heritage, as a young woman I spent time in worship and knew the power of God's presence, even as I walked through the valley of loneliness and desolation. That's why after making excuses for all the problems in my marriage, I would walk into the family room and play wor-ship music, which soothed my spirit and gave me strength to make it through the day.

I was not yet at the place my grandfather reached after my grandmother's warning. I still lived in the valley of excuses, telling myself that everything would be OK, that things would change. I made excuses about what was hap-pening behind closed doors, and I became an expert at hiding the truth from my loved ones and friends. I felt I could not tell my parents all that was going on and how much I was hurting because I knew they would tell me, "You must make a decision to change. No one can change the situation for you."

Because I wasn't ready for change, I went around the same mountain for sixteen years, until I realized that my life depended on my choosing to change. The seriousness of our marital situation was not just my husband's fault. I made mistakes too. However, the problems in our marriage were escalating to a point where I knew we had crossed the point of no return.

It was time for a change, and I knew it. Now, please don't misunderstand me. I'm not saying that if you're having problems in your marriage, you need to get up and leave. I won't share all that we faced in my situation, but my parents and I knew it was past time for me to do something.

One night I reached my breaking point, and I dialed my parents' number. "I can't do this anymore," I told them. "Will you come and help me move?"

There were no more excuses to be made. I could not lie enough, brag enough, or drink enough to cover all the pain and agony that were happening behind the closed doors of our home. Leaving that situation was the hardest thing I have done, but if I could have imagined how God would take me, mold me, and use me as He does today, I would have made my decision years earlier.

You can go from excuse making to change making too. Promises in the Word of God will give you the strength to do it. But are you ready for change? Moving from brokenness to a place of hope requires some decision making. It is up to you to forgive those who have wounded you and caused you such suffering—the parents who were absent when you needed them, the teacher who showed your entire class how incapable you were of measuring up, the friend who betrayed you, the family member who molested you, and even the pastor who hurt you.

LIFE IS BETTER WHEN YOU START FORGIVING THE PEOPLE WHO NEVER APOLOGIZED.
—@RealTalkKim

Don't hold on to your pain. You will only hurt yourself. It is time, *for your sake*, to forgive those who have wounded you and move on. Declare the following scriptures to help you let go of your hurts and move forward.

I can do all this through him who gives me strength.
—Philippians 4:13, niv

He gives strength to the weary and increases the power of the weak.

—ISAIAH 40:29, NIV

For if you forgive men their trespasses, your heavenly Father will also forgive you. But if you do not forgive men their trespasses, neither will your Father forgive your trespasses.

—MATTHEW 6:14–15

SUCCESS IS GETTING UP ONE MORE TIME THAN YOU FALL DOWN.
—*@RealTalkKim*

To become a strong man or woman who can make everyday decisions without faltering, you must release yourself from the shackles that have you bound. Your first steps might be a little shaky. You might even falter, but if you do, just get up. That's what success is—getting up one more time than you fall down.

Allow God to inspire you. Find your favorite scriptures. Get in worship. Move from where you are to where you want to be. As you let go of your pain, you will find solace in your healing. A healthy spirit brings a healthy body. Get active in doing things that you love to do. Look within during your prayer and meditation time each day. Seek out any remnants of unforgiveness and release them immediately.

Time's up. You are straight outta excuses!

> *Jesus, I submit myself to You and ask You to shine Your searchlight on my heart. Purify me from the inside out, and help me to be completely honest with myself. Give me strength each day to walk for You. Help me to forgive those who have wronged me. Amen.*

I DECLARE

I decree and declare that I will be free from my past and will reach out with expectation to my future. I will forgive others as my heavenly Father has forgiven me.

CHAPTER 8

BREAKING SOUL TIES

O N MY JOURNEY toward freedom there were times when I wondered if I knew anything about becoming free. I seemed to take one step toward God then two steps backward. Can you relate? Do you make a decision to change your circumstances, then revert to the old way of living when you face a challenge? Do you know it's time to let those old, partying friends go but when they come calling lose your resolve?

Do you feel as if you can't stay balanced on the scale of life? You're up, and you're down, all the while wondering why you can't just decide to change and then do it. You ask yourself, "Why is it so hard to live for God?" You know you want to move in the direction of God's purpose for your life, but something keeps dragging you back to your old ways. It seems impossible for you to get from where you are to the place where you're walking in your destiny.

You're not crazy, and you're not weak. I had to learn that sometimes we open doors in our lives that create ungodly soul ties. Those ties will keep us chained to past hurts and drag us back into bad habits and cycles. We have to learn to recognize and break those soul ties because if we don't, they will continually hold us hostage and rob us of freedom.

Let me explain. When I was seeking my spiritual

freedom, I began sensing in my spirit certain bondages from which I could not break free. Eventually I realized that because I had been involved in more than one physical relationship in my life, I remained connected to more than one partner.

When I realized these soul ties existed, I searched for ways to be free of them. I did not want to stay entangled in the past. Instead, I wanted to drop all excess baggage and find forgiveness for what I had allowed into my life. So I went to the Scriptures to hear what God was saying about willful sins and His way to freedom.

One biblical example gave me special understanding. It was the story of Abraham and Sarah. If you know about Abraham, you know he heard God's voice and is known as a man of great faith. When God promised him a son and many descendants through that son, Abraham got excited and looked forward to God's word coming to pass.

Abraham and his wife were not a young couple at the time. Nor was the promise of a child fulfilled quickly. In a culture that stressed childbearing as a woman's role, I cannot even imagine the frustration of being unable to conceive. It must have been very difficult for Sarah, and for Abraham, who loved her.

THE ONLY THING HARDER THAN WAITING ON GOD
IS WISHING YOU HAD.
—*@RealTalkKim*

Ten years went by, and still no baby. Sarah knew she was well beyond her childbearing years, so she proposed something that was considered customary for women who could not conceive:[1]

> Sarai said to Abram, "See now, the LORD has restrained me from bearing children. Please, go in

to my maid; perhaps I shall obtain children by her."
And Abram heeded the voice of Sarai.

—GENESIS 16:2

Abraham and Hagar came together, but the plan created more problems than peace. Scripture says that once she conceived, Hagar despised Sarah. Sarah also resented Hagar and treated her badly. Hagar ran away, but the angel of the Lord asked Hagar, "Where are you going?" (Gen. 16:8). When Hagar explained her situation, the angel of the Lord told her to return to Sarah. He promised that her son would become a great nation and said, "You shall call his name Ishmael, because the LORD has heard your affliction" (Gen. 16:11).[2]

God later brought forth Isaac, the child He promised in the first place. Isaac was born of the union of Abraham and Sarah, as God intended. But the situation was complicated, and tensions increased until Abraham sent away Hagar and Ishmael.

Much of the distress was caused by the soul tie formed when Abraham and Hagar had sexual relations. The bond they shared disrupted the family from that day forward. The chaos would have been avoided if Abraham and Sarah had waited and not tried to help God. As noted at GotQuestions.org:

> Sarah had no business offering her servant to Abraham, and Abraham had no business sleeping with Hagar. And Sarah was wrong to mistreat her servant as she did. Yet God worked through these situations. Hagar was blessed, and Abraham and Sarah were still the recipients of the promise. God's mercy is great, and His sovereign will is accomplished regardless of human frailty.[3]

By stepping ahead of God's promise, Abraham and Sarah opened the door to a triangle of soul ties. To walk in obedience and fulfill God's call on his life, Abraham had to sever the soul tie he had created with Hagar, which he did by sending her away.

Not all soul ties are negative, however. When God made Eve from Adam's rib, Adam said that Eve was flesh of his flesh and bone of his bone. (See Genesis 2:23.) They came from one flesh and were joined as one in spirit. A godly soul tie was formed in the marriage of the first human beings. It became the model of what we all desire in marriage. Yet the beneficial bond can become damaged by the ungodly actions of either party or both parties.

God has intended other types of godly soul ties to help build relationships among His children. If you have a friendship dating all the way back to your childhood, you and your friend have bonded in a way that few people understand. When others marvel at how close your family is in times of crisis, you know that you have a bond that is uncommon. In the midst of my life crisis the family bond I had always experienced was a soul tie that called me back to a security and rest I had always known.

WHEN I DISCOVERED SOUL TIES

As I journeyed back toward freedom, I realized that I needed to know more about soul ties so I could understand certain aspects of the oppression that had kept me bound all my life. I learned that a soul tie is a spirit or soul connection between two people who enter into a relationship. Whether the relationship is godly or ungodly is determined by the actions of those involved. For better or worse, the bond that is formed is not easily broken.

The problem with ungodly soul ties is that they normally occur when you disregard God's commands. There are times when such bonds are created by the sins of others. Most soul ties, however, are formed when you refuse to heed the still, small voice that lets you know you are headed in the wrong direction. Sometimes you also reject the cautions of those who have oversight and accountability concerning your life.

When I was in high school, I was best friends with a young lady who had a very controlling personality. I did not realize that she always decided our next move. Because my parents had committed themselves to providing a God-centered environment in our home, they covered my brother and me in prayer. They warned us about friends who were not helpful in our journey. I cannot tell you how many times my parents warned me about this particular friend. Yet I would not listen.

I knew she was not a Christian and did not even believe in God. Yet I would not break away from her. One day my parents instructed me to come home immediately after school, but this friend and I decided to go to the mall. Because she was the driver (in the relationship and in her vehicle), I did whatever she suggested and faced the consequences for my actions later.

That day we were involved in a severe accident that would change the trajectory of our friendship. I was taken to one hospital as she was airlifted to a trauma center in critical condition. I was able to be released that day, but my friend remained several weeks in the critical care unit, hovering between life and death.

After she recovered, it was as though our friendship had never existed. It was as if it had been blotted out of her memory. Can I explain what happened? Absolutely not. But the relationship that I felt was the most important part of my life became only a memory.

As I said previously, sometimes a person's rejection is God's protection. Not until many years later did I realize that in my immaturity I had surrendered my identity and become whoever my friend wanted me to be. This is how ungodly soul ties can form in a person's life.

Only after returning to my parents' home at thirty-six years of age did I realize that through the years I had allowed myself to be controlled by spirits that were not of God. I saw myself as so strong and independent and capable of calling the shots for my own life, but many times I allowed others to determine my success or failure. Those relationships were not edifying me, building me up, or giving me peace. At that time in my life I was in a state of confusion, trying to prove my value to anyone who would listen. Ungodly soul ties had produced a harvest of bad fruit, not only for me but also for my children.

> **GOD OFTEN REMOVES PEOPLE FROM YOUR LIFE FOR A REASON.**
> **THINK BEFORE YOU CHASE AFTER THEM.**
> —*@RealTalkKim*

FREEDOM FROM SOUL TIES

As I began dealing with my ungodly soul ties, I realized how badly I needed to be delivered from the fruit of my choices. So I did some research, learned what God's Word says about the issue, and discovered some steps I needed to take. If you are in a similar situation, these steps will help you too.

Choose to change.

When confusion and disarray show up in your life, something has to change. "For God is not the author of confusion but of peace" (1 Cor. 14:33).

Because I had been raised by godly parents who taught me to seek the Lord, I could not be content in any ungodly relationship, no matter how hard I tried. In fact, I was miserable—always feeling uneasy, extremely anxious, and afraid. I cannot remember how many times I declared that I would make a change. Yet I didn't. Instead, I would hang out with the same friends the very next day. I was connected by unholy soul ties that were destroying me and my family.

David's words fit my situation: "I am feeble and severely broken; I groan because of the turmoil of my heart" (Ps. 38:8). Even though David truly loved God, he created unholy soul ties that ultimately made him miserable. As he poured out his heart in this psalm, he came face to face with his sins and the sickness caused by his actions.

Years ago, as I read David's words, I understood the pain and anguish he felt. I sensed the weight of his baggage because I had a lifetime of baggage that needed to be purged. I wondered how I could release myself from years of bad decisions, and how the desire to change could lead to the moves that would set me free.

All I could do was dig deeper in the Word of God, read whatever I could find on soul ties, listen to preachers describe how illicit relationships start, and find out how to break those bondages. What I needed was deliverance from what had taken me hostage, and I was determined to find it.

Seek godly counseling.

In my search I discovered amazing insights in the Book of Proverbs and took them personally. I was stunned at how many times Solomon spoke about our need for people who can counsel us and help lead us to safety.

> Where there is no counsel, the people fall; but in the multitude of counselors there is safety.
> —PROVERBS 11:14

> Without counsel, plans go awry, but in the multitude of counselors they are established.
> —PROVERBS 15:22

> For by wise counsel you will wage your own war, and in a multitude of counselors there is safety.
> —PROVERBS 24:6

These verses helped me realize that my hope was in God. I was a living example of plans going awry. At eighteen I left home, much like the prodigal son in Luke 15, who wanted a partying lifestyle. As young as I was, I thought I knew more than my parents could ever tell me. I refused instruction and found myself back in their home eighteen years later.

The prodigal's story resonated with me. He spent all his inheritance with so-called friends, who rejected him when his money was gone. Penniless, he found himself in a pigpen feeding the animals, while he went hungry. No Hebrew could imagine himself in such a place! Homeless and at the end of himself, he thought about the servants in his father's home. They had more than he did and were well fed.

Finally it dawned on him: "Why not go back, repent, and become a servant at my father's house?" He knew he did not deserve anything more than that. Of course, at the end of the prodigal account we read that his father had been waiting for him the whole time. When the prodigal got home, his father welcomed him back into the family with open arms, not as a servant but a son.

I remember one day being overcome by the thought of how my parents, who had always been there for me, kept wanting me to return to the family. Through the years, I continually chose my friends over them, even on holidays. I was too busy, had prior commitments, or did not feel like making the trip. I always found some reason to stay away. Then, like a true prodigal, I was back in their home, broken, miserable, and needing solace for my sons and myself.

To become free from the many decisions that had caused so much pain, I needed to do more than say, "I'm sorry." I was weighed down with the troubles I chose to pack in my baggage. Now I was ready to unload all of it. Everything that had me bound had to go. Spiritual deliverance from the evil spirits I'd inadvertently welcomed into my life was an absolute must.

On the day I was to meet with a pastor who would guide me through my deliverance, I asked God to lead me in every decision I would make that day. I went into the session knowing I was a willing participant, and I would be set free. The pastor began by praying that I would be honest with him and with myself. To be free, I would have to admit that I had sinned. Once I did, his godly counsel could follow.

Repent.

Once you face your sins, it is time to release them in the name of Jesus Christ. Ask the Lord to bring to your remembrance all the illicit relationships and soul ties you have allowed. You cannot break what binds you if you cover up or deny your choices and the doors you have opened. Only you can decide to face your true self. There might be some pain involved, but just allow the Holy Spirit to deal with your emotions. He will see you through.

Declare in the name of the Lord Jesus that you are cutting off any ungodly soul ties formed between you and anyone else. This includes those "created by any relationship, sexual or otherwise, known or unknown, remembered or forgotten," as a wonderful prayer to break soul ties states.[4]

Accept forgiveness.

We have talked quite a bit about forgiveness, but forgiveness is not just for others. It is for you too. By faith accept the covering of the blood of Jesus Christ that has washed you white as snow. You need not allow the sins of your past to resurface *ever again*. You don't need to be ruled by your emotions any longer. You are a child of God who has every right to approach His throne as one whose sins are paid in full.

Look to God.

When your deliverance seems far away, let Jesus' words comfort you: "Peace I leave with you, My peace I give to you; not as the world gives do I give to you. Let not your heart be troubled, neither let it be afraid" (John 14:27).

After being tormented by the cares of life and the soul ties you have formed, it is comforting to walk in a peace you cannot explain or understand. Paul speaks about this peace in Philippians 4:7 when he says it "will guard your hearts and minds through Christ Jesus."

That peace is available, and obtaining it is simply a matter of accepting God's forgiveness. I had never realized that even in the worst of challenges, a child of God can be at peace. That was not something I had ever experienced. I always stayed one step ahead of God (or so I thought), working out my situations and thinking I could handle every challenge. If I couldn't, I would call my parents, who always seemed to have the right answer at the right time.

However, when I was losing my marriage, home, business, and family unit, my parents could not put my broken heart back together or heal the bleeding wounds of my devastated little boys. My sons needed their parents' care, but my husband and I were too busy fighting and creating havoc to understand their pain. So my parents assisted by bringing us back into their home.

Nevertheless, we needed other things that only God could give. As Joyce Meyer famously says, the battlefield is in your mind.[5] That is where Satan attacks! During the battle to keep my marriage and life as I had known them, I began experiencing severe headaches that would render me helpless. My family and I were in the mall one day when I felt a severe pain in my head and fell to the floor.

In a state of disbelief, I struggled to comprehend what was happening. I could hear my husband telling me to get up, but I couldn't move, so I became even more afraid that I was having a stroke or even dying. I was rushed to the emergency room, which led to months of testing but provided no answers about my condition. Each day, I feared that one of these episodes would destroy me. I knew there had to be an answer, and it must be spiritual.

Finally I sought God for an answer about why the doctors could not find whatever was causing my debilitating pain. As I asked Him to expose the source of the challenge, I also questioned why I had yet another situation to battle. The Lord allowed me to see that it was an attack by Satan.

At that time I had no idea that God had a purpose for my life unlike anything I could imagine. I was so broken and so far from His presence that I only sought Him during emergencies. Yet I always knew where to go when I needed Him. I would fall down in my living room with worship music blaring throughout my house, and I would cry out for mercy. However, I was a selfish daughter who only came to her heavenly Father when she could no longer accomplish life without Him.

WHAT GOD HAS PLACED UPON YOU IS GREATER THAN THE HELL THAT WAS PLACED AGAINST YOU.
—*@RealTalkKim*

During a certain visit with my parents, my head began to throb, and I sensed another attack coming. I had been standing for freedom and knew this pain was meant to steal my peace. I had to take back what Satan was trying to steal from me! At that moment, as I paced the room and cried out to God, my husband walked in the room. Immediately I yelled out to him, "Pray or get out!"

He was out of that room before I could even process his departure. I can tell you that God set me free that day. I have never had that type of challenge since that day.

Make Jesus the Lord of your life and thoughts.

I had allowed so many unholy relationships in my life that I knew I had to take back whatever ground Satan had stolen from me. That meant knocking down everything that defied the truth of God's Word by "casting down arguments and every high thing that exalts itself against the knowledge of God, bringing every thought into captivity to the obedience of Christ" (2 Cor. 10:5).

This was important because your thoughts determine your actions. I knew there was a battle going on in my mind, and I knew that only I could determine my outcome. Casting down imaginations and bringing my mind into line with Christ would not happen overnight, or even in a week or month. I just knew that it was a necessary step in my journey of freedom.

First I acknowledged Jesus as Lord of my entire life. Then I began taking my thoughts captive and realizing that I could choose to have the mind of Christ. I believed that I could change my world by changing my mind. Changing my mind then changed every word I said.

"Death and life are in the power of the tongue, and those who love it will eat its fruit" (Prov. 18:21). This scripture is one that I not only quote daily but preach about weekly. In coming to freedom, I realize that I have totally changed my vocabulary. My dad always said, "You can't keep birds from flying over your head, but you can keep them from building a nest there." (Other preachers have made similar statements.) It's true of birds, and it's true of negative thoughts.

GOD IS ALWAYS READY TO MOVE
WHEN YOU DECIDE THAT IT IS TIME TO BE FREE.
—@RealTalkKim

Because you are a spirit living in a human body and dealing with flesh daily, you will have to deal with negative thoughts. Remember that the enemy is the god of this atmosphere and will do whatever is necessary to keep you from being focused on freedom. It is up to you to cast down those thoughts and fill your mind and spirit man with the Word of God.

God is always ready to move when you decide that it is time to be free. It's up to you to determine when you are ready for deliverance and ready to break all soul ties in your life. I knew I was full of disobedience because everything I touched was cursed. My business, which had been so blessed, began to fall apart. My marriage, which had been my greatest accomplishment, was on life support. Even physically I knew that I had to change.

I had been caught up in my selfishness and afraid that if I walked in God's will, I would have to walk alone. The idea of being alone made me afraid. I had so changed myself to please others that I did not even know myself. So I kept submitting my life to God, only to step back and refuse His guidance. When my husband would just leave our home and family, sometimes for weeks at a time, I would immediately find a church and get my family involved. When he returned, I felt I no longer needed church fellowship. This had become a familiar scene in our home, so my boys and I were not surprised when he left or when he came back. We were on a vicious cycle, and clearly something needed to change.

WHAT A DIFFERENCE A CHANGE MAKES!

Only when I completely lost my earthly treasures and marriage did I finally realize that partial obedience is disobedience. As far as I could tell, my life was over. But when I stopped running from His guidance and decided I truly wanted to change, with no turning back to my old ways, God began to move in my life.

Now, eleven years later, I am more fulfilled and blessed than I ever thought possible. I am a living epistle read of all men. (See 2 Corinthians 3:2.) Since breaking free from soul ties, I have experienced a peace that transcends understanding. My sleep is more restful than it had been for many years, and my life is no longer full of confusion.

I have also found a love that I never dreamed possible. Honor is now my best friend. I spend quality time with my family and let everyone know that after my husband, Mark, my parents are my best friends.

How I wish I could take away your pain and release you from the burdens you are carrying. But I cannot. The Lord is your answer. He is no respecter of persons. You *can* be set free from the bondages that have imprisoned you. You can move into a new realm of faith that will keep you in perfect peace in every area of your life. He said He would never leave you or forsake you. He will be with you until the very end. Now it is up to you. Let this chapter's closing prayer move you toward the freedom you desire!

> *Jesus, break every chain that binds me in the ungodly soul ties that have been formed out of past relationships. I now accept Your forgiveness and peace in the name of the Lord Jesus Christ. Amen.*

I DECLARE

I decree and declare that I am free from any ungodly soul tie that has kept me bound to sin. I release every hurt and pain caused by ungodly relationships, and I now move from brokenness into total freedom. I am a child of God covered by the blood of Jesus. No weapon formed against me shall prosper.

CHAPTER 9

STOP PRESSING REWIND!
HIT DELETE!

BY NOW YOU know that I am an authority on the art of feeling stuck! Even my parents can testify about how I orchestrated situations in my early childhood that left me feeling as if I'd built an impenetrable wall around myself.

When I was three, my parents pastored a new, upstart church while dealing with their very strong-willed little girl. One Sunday evening they decided they could no longer fight me, so they brought me to the altar and prayed that I would be released from the spirit of agitation that was harassing not only me but also my parents. My parents were realizing I was a child who would need constant direction to learn to use her strong will for good.

Each night at bedtime my parents would tenderly lay me in my beautiful canopy bed, pray over me, read me a Bible story, turn out the light, and whisper, "Good night." Then they would walk across the hall, close their bedroom door behind them, and get ready for sleep.

Within ten minutes I would leave my bed and lie on the floor outside their bedroom door, screaming and sobbing until they allowed me into their bed to sleep between them. This pattern continued for such a long time that no matter what situation we faced, I always got my way. I am not recommending tantrum throwing. I am only reporting that it worked, to a point.

Over time I came to realize that my strong will needed to be used in healthier ways. I developed a determination to use that strong will for the glory of the kingdom. So in my most trying times, I refuse to allow the enemy to steal my joy. That joy came at a very high price: it cost me thirty-six years of trying to do it on my own to show the world I could make it, then falling lower than I could ever have imagined. But the story didn't end there, because I allowed God to pick me up, mold me, and make me into His vessel.

The truth is that exerting your will has its place. When you get stuck in circumstances that keep you from your God-given potential, you have to develop the will to push past your "stuckness."

HELPING GOD HELP ME

When I was in first grade, my mother drove me to school each day, even though I could easily have taken the bus. The problem was that I did not want to be separated from my mother for hours at a time. That's how insecure and alone I felt. So when we arrived at school, I would scream and sob, fighting not to get out of the car. The principal would have to come and help my mom get me to class.

My parents seemed to know how to handle everyone else's challenges but could not figure out what to do with me, the little girl who would never be like other children. I told you about my learning difficulties and how my teacher used to embarrass and criticize me in front of my classmates. When the principal found out about it, he started keeping me in his office for several hours each day. This continued until our family moved to another city to start another church.

After we moved, my mother waited a week before making an appointment with my new teacher. The teacher already sensed that something was amiss and requested my parents' agreement to order some psychological testing. That ultimately led to my being branded "learning disabled" and enrolled in seven years of summer school and tutoring.

My parents always looked for teachers and school programs that could provide me a first-rate education. When I was in the seventh grade, they enrolled my brother and me in a very popular Christian school with about five hundred students.

This proved to be a difficult turning point for me. My parents chose the school because it had a class for students with learning problems. When I walked in on the first day, I saw students drooling and making unusual gestures. The scene was foreign to me. Suddenly I realized that being "special" meant being set apart from most of the student body. I remember looking out the window and seeing my brother and his friends changing classes, playing volleyball, and going to lunch. Then our little class would join hands and walk together to the lunchroom, where some of the students would have to be fed the way babies are fed.

I had always thought that I was a smart, funny, balanced kid. However, the longer I stayed in that class, the more I questioned my sanity. "Maybe I'm drooling and don't know it," I thought. "Maybe I think I'm normal, but I'm this other kind of special."

These thoughts weighed on me. I got so quiet that my parents would ask, "Has someone hurt you? Are the other kids being mean to you?"

When I couldn't take it any longer, I told my parents how I felt. I explained that I looked and acted normal, yet I was in a class with kids whose challenges seemed much more serious than mine. I wondered whether my parents knew something that I didn't know. Was I less functional than I realized? Did I not understand how broken I was?

My parents began weeping and explaining that because of

my learning disability, they thought a Christian school with a "custom" class was best for me. At that point they realized that it was destroying my self-esteem. Being in that class made me feel so much like a loser that I no longer believed in myself.

My parents immediately withdrew me from the school and transferred me back to public school. However, I was still in a class for the learning disabled. I knew in my gut that I did not need that type of help, so I asked my parents to give me a chance to prove it. I was tired of being labeled, and I believed I could make it in regular classes. It would mean letting God help me. So my parents and I prayed for God to give us wisdom to make the right decisions for my future.

When I entered high school, they merged me into regular classes—not college preparatory classes like my brother was in but classes that included assistance in my job search after graduation. Finally I deleted the learning-disabled label! Some quirky things happened, such as when I flunked typing in school but passed a typing test at a job consulting firm. Some amazing things happened, such as when I became the president of the Future Business Leaders Club. At the time, I was going to school full time *and* working a full-time job. I even purchased my own BMW during this time! The point is that I refused to allow people's perceptions of me to keep me stuck.

DON'T EVER ALLOW SOMEONE'S SHALLOW PERCEPTION OF YOU DETERMINE THE DEPTH OF WHAT YOU HAVE TO OFFER. GOD MADE YOU UNIQUELY EXTRAORDINARY.
—*@RealTalkKim*

This was only one of many situations I had to press through, and it forced me to change. I had to help God help me. To succeed in regular classes, I had to participate in class. That meant being willing to work harder.

Are you getting my point? Your situations and labels may be different from mine, but the ways you get free are similar. I have learned in my "life college" that class participation is a necessary prerequisite to freedom. I have to act. In other words, I have to cooperate with what God is doing in my life.

I must also give credit where credit is due. My mom sat with me for hours each night as I studied spelling words, math problems, and short stories. I still struggled with retention, so my mom reviewed the previous day's material by asking me questions the next morning. I sometimes had problems remembering what we had studied, yet my mom never let me see her frustration.

Looking back, I can see that God really does have a sense of humor. Watching myself preaching on YouTube and quoting scriptures that I have memorized proves that He is a miracle worker too. As a young student, I could not remember ten spelling words for my Friday test, but I now have numerous sermons in my head and have authored four books.

Who could have imagined it? I was stuck for a long time, but as I grasped God's plan for me, I did not allow the enemy to steal it.

TAKE A STEP

Because I allowed God to help me move out of my learning-disabled "prison," I learned how to break out of many more. I could have kept allowing the enemy to remind me about my insecurities and lack of self-esteem. If I did, he would control every facet of my life.

It is totally up to us to experience change. Jesus made that clear to the man at the pool of Bethesda. He had been in a life-limiting situation for thirty-eight years. Honestly his condition was much more difficult than what I faced. He was unable to get around on his own and suffered failure after failure because he had no help. The apostle John explains his story:

> There is in Jerusalem by the Sheep Gate a pool, which is called in Hebrew, Bethesda, having five porches. In these lay a great multitude of sick people, blind, lame, paralyzed, waiting for the moving of the water. For an angel went down at a certain time into the pool and stirred up the water; then whoever stepped in first, after the stirring of the water, was made well of whatever disease he had.
>
> Now a certain man was there who had an infirmity thirty-eight years. When Jesus saw him lying there, and knew that he already had been in that condition a long time, He said to him, "Do you want to be made well?" The sick man answered Him, "Sir, I have no man to put me into the pool when the water is stirred up; but while I am coming, another steps down before me." Jesus said to him, "Rise, take up your bed and walk." And immediately the man was made well, took up his bed, and walked. And that day was the Sabbath.
>
> —JOHN 5:2–9

Jesus went to Jerusalem during the Passover and visited the pool of Bethesda. The Bible says that when an angel stirred the water in the pool, the first person to get in would be completely healed. There were many needy people waiting for their moment. They all wanted to be the first one in the water, but only one person could be the first.

On this particular day, the infirm man was healed—but why?

He was ready to be made whole.

After thirty-eight years of infirmity the man was ready to be free. There was no one in his life to assist him in taking the necessary steps. Yet I believe he had reached a point at which he would do whatever was required for his healing.

I cannot help but wonder how many times he'd lost all hope of ever being made whole. Maybe he wavered between hope and hopelessness, I don't know. However, after thirty-eight years I would think he felt totally stuck in his situation.

He was ready to act on his faith.

After thirty-eight years I believe the infirm man was ready to accept assistance from anyone who was willing to give it. All it took was allowing Jesus into His life and acting on his faith when Jesus instructed him to rise and take up his bed. The man immediately got up and walked. It was his choice to make, and he made it.

During my journey to getting unstuck, my ups and downs were a lot like those of the infirm man. I went through times of discouragement and times when I believed my situation would change. Eventually I realized that God was ready to assist me in my deliverance. So I added action to my prayers and did whatever was necessary to move out of my present situation and into that place of change. I wanted to be made whole.

DELETE WHAT STINKS

I remember traveling with my parents to Pensacola, Florida, where they had been invited to speak. As we entered a small town named Cantonment, my brother and I detected a foul odor and mentioned it to my parents, who also noticed it.

We all held our noses and gasped for air as we pulled into a gas station. When we asked the attendant about the smell, he acted as though it was nothing out of the ordinary. We were amazed and tried telling him how horrible the smell was. Finally the attendant remembered that there was a paper mill down the street. Everyone in town had become so accustomed to the odor created by the mill that they didn't notice it anymore. The mill provided a good living for them, so they learned to live with it. Eventually we got used to it too.

Through my years growing up in a preacher's family, I visited with friends whose family environment was much different from mine. Quarreling was a normal, everyday affair in their house, but it made me very uncomfortable. I was not accustomed to this type of behavior, but they were.

They were like the people who no longer noticed the odor from the paper mill. I wondered how they could live that way and not cry out for help. Until I became broken and homeless, I did not realize how easily we learn to accept our dysfunction. I had no idea that I would one day be stuck in a similar cycle, having to decide whether to accept life as it was or change it.

If you want to get unstuck, you must identify what stinks, realize there is a way out, and start deleting what no longer fits. That means shaking off complacency and believing that when you decide it's time for a change, change will come.

If I had waited for other people to decide that I could be integrated into the regular high school population, it never would have happened. My student transcript showed that there was a definite problem from elementary all the way through middle school. Why would they even try to promote me to another level?

WHEN YOU DECIDE IT'S TIME FOR A CHANGE, CHANGE WILL COME.
—*@RealTalkKim*

My parents had to interrupt the "usual flow" before administrators would allow me to prove my ability. I had no proof to offer them, but a lion inside of me was ready to be unleashed. I knew that God had never made a nobody, and the greatness within me was ready to shine. I refused to be saddled with labels, especially old ones. It was time for me to stop rewinding and press "Delete."

This bears repeating: to move forward, I had to quit making excuses and blaming others. I could never have gotten unstuck by trying to shift blame for my difficulties. The blame game would only have moved me deeper into complacency.

GROWTH TAKES TIME

My parents could not have known for certain how my life would turn out. They knew, however, that they had always prayed over my brother and me. In fact, while building our church, my dad was out several nights a week for in-family Bible studies. My mom made good use of that time. She had us kids sit together, read the Bible, and pray together. We didn't really want to do it, but Mom knew it would help keep us grounded.

I was still strong-willed and continued to test my parents during my middle school and high school years. No one could figure out why I was so critical and unable to get along with others. My parents longed for us to become consecrated Christians. Yet I did whatever I could to disrupt the flow. For example, after praying and reading the Bible with my mom, I would go to bed with rock-and-roll music in my ears.

I had no idea that my mom came into my room in the middle of the night to cut off the rock music and pray over me. She and my dad asked God for His solution to my resistance. Finally my mom had the bright idea to connect speakers throughout our house. At seven each morning I was awakened to the booming sound of praise-and-worship music being piped throughout the house.

Being jolted from sleep at that hour made me furious. My mom just laughed and let me know that she was protecting my brother and me from ourselves. She was right. It was a critical time, and my parents had spiritual insight into my future. They were like the angel at the pool of Bethesda, stirring the water for miracles. Their vigilance helped to establish a path forward for me. Their efforts helped prepare me for life's turns.

As you read these pages, I pray you let Jesus guide you in deleting whatever needs to go from your life. The choice is simple. You can keep replaying your mistakes, or you can press "Delete." First you have to intentionally accept God's plan for your life and realize that choices must be made for change to happen.

The man at the pool of Bethesda had to choose to believe. Jesus did not tell him to get into the pool. He simply asked if he wanted to be made well. When Jesus told him to rise, take up his bed, and walk, the man had only to obey!

"As many as are led by the Spirit of God, these are sons of God" (Rom. 8:14). There are times when, in our dullness of hearing or our weariness with warring, someone suggests something we had not previously considered. I believe that is what happened to the man at the pool of Bethesda. He had been waiting for someone to have mercy on him. The battle had worn him down. He kept pressing "Rewind" because being stuck was all he had known for thirty-eight years. Then Jesus asked a potentially life-changing question.

The man's past could have defined his future for another four decades. It didn't. He listened to Jesus and followed His instructions. That simple act revolutionized his life!

Jesus, I am ready to take up my bed and walk. I am tired of being crippled by my choices and life's challenges. I ask You to give me direction and wisdom to make wise choices as I allow You to be Lord of my life. Amen.

I DECLARE

I decree and declare that I am moving from where I am to where You want me to be. I release everyone who has kept me bound, and I accept my destiny to become the person You purposed me to become.

PART III

SHIFTING FROM YOUR BAD TO HIS GOOD

When God grants you His favor, nothing can stop the blessings He has in store!

CHAPTER 10

FUMIGATE

H AVE YOU EVER heard anyone say, "Just get over it," "Don't let your past rule you," "Become aggressive in your recovery," or "Take back what the enemy has stolen from you"? Those words sound good and are often said by well-meaning individuals, but beginning a journey toward transformation is rarely that simple. That's because changing may mean you have to get rid of the old to prepare for the new. In other words, sometimes things must change so you can change and take hold of what God has for you.

To enter the next season of your life, you must determine that it's time to decontaminate and clean some things out of your life. No matter how tired you are of being where you are, no one can do this for you. To experience lasting change, you must go through the process of clearing your mind of the lies that keep you holding on to hurts, bad habits, and addictive behaviors. You must let go of the negative thoughts that have caused you to lose more ground in your past than you have gained. In short, you must fumigate.

When you fumigate you "disinfect, purify, sterilize, sanitize, decontaminate, [or] cleanse," to use some common synonyms.[1] I do this once each quarter at my house. A young man shows up and sprays the inside of our house with insecticide. I used to wonder why the spray was necessary, since no bugs had infiltrated our home. I wasn't trying to be difficult; I just had nagging concerns about insecticides being dangerous. So at one point I instructed my exterminator to spray only the outside of the house.

Then I started seeing creatures so small I wasn't sure they were actually there. First there was one in the guest bathtub; then I saw a squiggly little thing that was looking for a new home on my bathroom floor. The next time the exterminator came, I was a little embarrassed that I was seeing bugs and asked him to spray inside again. I said, "I know my home stays neat and clean. So where did the bugs come from?"

He laughingly let me know I was not seeing bugs because I kept a dirty house. He told me that if a bathtub isn't used regularly, the pipes become dry and serve as an easy access point for underground pests looking for an indoor home. To keep them out, he instructed me to run water weekly through all my sinks and bathtubs.

Are you getting the idea? There is a similar process in the spiritual realm, and it's a huge part of how you live abundantly and enter new seasons. To keep out the "bugs" that try to infiltrate your mind, you must stay connected to the Holy Spirit and let the water of God's Word renew your mind daily. This must become part of your lifestyle because just as pesky bugs return even after the exterminator visits, the baggage we let go of can also begin to resurface if we do not continually keep our minds focused on Jesus.

The people I meet each week are on different levels where fumigating is concerned. Many are crying out for help. Some cannot stop the angry outbursts and irritation caused by family members or dysfunctional relationships. Others carry such a heavy load of resentment and bitterness that it is difficult for them to spend time in the Lord's presence. Confusion is so ruling their lives that they feel cut off from the peace of God. Still others cannot forgive themselves for what they have allowed to happen in their lifetimes.

A friend who just can't seem to release his hurt and pain

explained how he feels. Throughout his life his parents heaped verbal abuse on him. Now in times of trouble he lashes out at the people closest to him. He wants to change. He certainly does not want to hurt his loved ones, and he knows he is driving them away.

When I told him that fumigating meant he would have to choose to change his thinking, he said he could not get his father's voice out of his head. That voice kept telling him he would *never* measure up; he would *never* hit the mark. My friend had lived in the shadow of his critics so long that he believed it when they said he would never be good enough. No matter what he did, no matter how much he accomplished, he could not satisfy them. He therefore concluded that he had tried every possible way to move forward—counselors, self-help books, you name it—but could never be free.

He was believing more lies from the enemy. I couldn't seem to convince him that taking in all that mental "junk" instead of cleaning it out would just keep him stuck repeating the same negative patterns he said he wanted to be free from.

It is heartbreaking and completely understandable to see how stuck we can get. That is where the analogy of the dry bathroom pipes comes in. Running the water keeps unwelcome intruders from gathering. Most of the time you don't even know they are there until they come out in the open. The same is true of attitudes and mind-sets that congregate and show themselves at the most unexpected times in your spiritual experience.

Bad memories can leave scars so deep that even when you recognize them, you do not know how to release them. Being a Christian does not mean that you will automatically be free from painful memories. You have to deal with everything that haunts you in your present life, and you have to make good memories to replace and overcome your past hurts.

I once counseled a young man who was lacking direction and focus in his life. His family had been full of strife and he'd been told he would be just like his dad and never amount to much in life. I told him he was allowing his heritage to consume him to the point that he had submitted to the rule of a past he cannot change. I explained that he shouldn't allow his youthful victimhood to label his adult life and his memories don't have to haunt him forever.

Yet as we talked, he lashed out. He said he knew he would never be worth anything and would always be like his worthless dad. "So why," he asked, "should I try to change what cannot be fixed?"

Can you see how this young man was allowing his family background to determine his future? He had become so accustomed to brokenness that he began to use it as a crutch for why he doesn't keep a job or accomplish anything in life. Until he releases the shackles that have him bound, he cannot move forward.

YOU NEED A TEAM

When you're ready to fumigate, honesty is the best policy. Look in the mirror and acknowledge what you see. Then get after it. It does you no good to purchase books and CDs just to get information. You need to use information to make the necessary changes to grow spiritually. Once you decide that you are going to make a change, you can ask for help and invite others to walk with you—trusted friends who can help you grow closer to God.

Jesus could have walked the earth alone, but He didn't. The almighty God had manifested in the flesh and did not need anyone to be an extension of Himself. He had the power to set men free, heal the sick, and even raise the dead. So why did He choose twelve uneducated men (including fishermen and tax collectors) to be on His team?

Jesus and these men were together day and night, walking the villages and countryside, doing good for others. He poured Himself into them continually, sharing His beliefs, faith, and direction. He regularly excused Himself from their presence and found places of solitude to pray to the Father. When He was in the Garden of Gethsemane and He knew His crucifixion was on the horizon, He asked His trusted friends to stay awake and pray with Him. They were His team.

To experience release in your life, you need people you can trust to assist you through your growth process, to stand with you as you release the things that have kept you bound. It can't be just anybody. You have to surround yourself with people who can handle their roles in your transition times.

SOMETIMES THE OBSTACLES THAT NEED TO BE REMOVED FROM YOUR LIFE HAVE NAMES.
—*@RealTalkKim*

Take a sober look around you. Are the people influencing you the most actually toxic? Pay attention to who is affecting you more negatively than positively. If you want to enter a new season, you might have to release those who were there through your previous failures. They might not be ready to move into the new season you want to enter. If they hesitate to be part of the change because they are firmly planted in the status quo, they will hold you back. Even if they did not seem toxic before, they become toxic to you now.

Face it: toxic relationships and environments will do nothing but suck the life out of you.

TRANSFORMATION IS A PROCESS

Paul told us, "Do not be conformed to this world, but be transformed by the renewing of your mind, that you may prove what is that good and acceptable and perfect will of God" (Rom. 12:2). The word Paul used for *transformed* is the

Greek word we use for describing the metamorphosis of a butterfly.

We love to see butterflies in our gardens but rarely think about what it took for them to become the beautiful creatures before us. Butterflies begin as eggs and become caterpillars, which can eat their way through entire gardens and whole forests. They can cause enough devastation to upset the ecological balance and threaten their own existence.

Through metamorphosis, however, caterpillars become totally different creatures. The change is a great picture of how the renewed mind totally transforms us. A change of mind alters our thinking processes in relation to God and His standards. In Christ our thoughts become brand-new. When that happens, we quit defending ourselves and enter the process of surrender that allows metamorphosis to take place.

Notice that I said *in Christ* we become brand-new. You can change your mind about many things, but to become a new creation in Christ Jesus, you must pursue a true and personal relationship with Him. As you seek God and surrender to Him, you let go of your own ways and mind-sets and learn to see from God's point of view. The way He sees things becomes the way you see them. As you do this daily and walk in His presence, you develop the mind of Christ. You can get rid of that bipolar spiritual mentality that causes you to be up one day and down the next. You will no longer flutter from one decision to the next, not really knowing your own mind.

Paul said that "if anyone is in Christ, he is a new creation; old things have passed away; behold, all things have become new" (2 Cor. 5:17). That is true. Yet you can read that verse daily and still not discard your old way of thinking. Becoming a new creation is more than accepting Jesus as Lord. It is an ongoing journey of choosing to make Him Lord.

Do you know people who are up and down spiritually?

They are on fire one Sunday and sitting on the back pew the next because they "don't feel like" participating. They offend people with their "wit" and then say, "Just kidding." Unfortunately the damage is done, and friendships are lost. They call themselves "Christians," but nothing about them seems brand-new. They need to renew their minds!

You cannot make anyone change. You do, however, have the power to allow change in yourself. Jesus Christ will not force you to be transformed. You must decide to cooperate with Him in your metamorphosis process. I always say that I want to be pliable like a willow, not shaking in the wind like a reed. Even when the willow bends under pressure, it rises again. When a reed bends in the storm, it breaks.

YOU CANNOT LIVE A VICTORIOUS LIFE
IF YOU TAKE THE PAST WITH YOU.
—@RealTalkKim

If you renew your mind, you will be transformed. Let's take a look at some of the benefits of transformation.

You become brand-new.

When old things are passing away, you can live a brand-new life. It is time to empty the old baggage. Toss out the pain of criticism or the tendency to manipulate. Let God run you through His washer and bring you out sparkling clean. He'll give you a new slate because He forgives your sins, never to remember them again. Oh, you can become a Christian and keep the old baggage if you choose, but you cannot live a victorious life if you take the past with you.

God works with you.

What is your part in growing? You already know it's not all about you trying harder but about cooperating with God. He gave His Son, who is the Word. Receiving the Son and renewing your mind through the Word are *your* part. (See Romans 10:13; 12:1–2; and Philippians 4:8–9.)

When I was in school, at one point I felt as though I would never graduate. My mom worked with me for hours as I did my homework and studied for tests. However, she never did my assignments for me. I think that is what we expect when we ask God to renew our minds. He will not do our work for us. He has given us His Word, but it is up to us to feed on it. He will do His part, but He will not do ours.

God provides the power of a sound mind.

When fear and intimidation try to bind you, remember, the Bible says, "For God has not given us a spirit of fear, but of power and of love and of a sound mind" (2 Tim. 1:7). This is a scripture I recite daily. The power I have to see people set free from bondages and chains in my weekly meetings comes only through my daily process of renewing my mind while releasing everything that tries to bind me. I'm no different than you when dealing with life's situations. I too pop off at the mouth when I should be exercising control. I too mess up many times in my relationships, yet I know that God promised me a sound mind.

In moments of stress, pressure, or fear, have you been tempted to cry out that you were losing your mind? That it's just too much pressure? Do you feel as if you can't take any more stress? If so, don't worry. You won't lose your mind. God's Word declares you have a sound mind that works in the most challenging situations. Again, I must tell you that you cannot know the power of the Word of God unless you get into the Word and know its contents. His Word is truly our medicine.

The enemy is always looking for ways to distract and worry you. Don't worry! He cannot beat the mind of Christ in you. Nothing is impossible with God, but the enemy will not step aside and give you a pass. He will try every trick in his book to keep you under the weight of fear and stress. Your job is to stay focused in God's presence. That is what Jesus did. Let Him be your example. Take breaks by getting away in the presence of God.

THE DEVIL HAD A PLOT, BUT GOD HAS A PLAN.
HOLD ON. IT AIN'T OVER!
—@RealTalkKim

In your darkest season you have the promise of peace and of knowing that the Spirit of truth will direct you. Jesus said that "when He, the Spirit of truth, has come, He will guide you into all truth; for He will not speak on His own authority, but whatever He hears He will speak; and He will tell you things to come" (John 16:13).

Jesus' words show us that while darkness is pervasive in the world, He has come as the light. We can be tempted to search for truth and light in so many other places, but none of them will give us hope. Jesus, the only true light, is our hope.

God provides wisdom.

"If any of you lacks wisdom, let him ask of God, who gives to all liberally and without reproach, and it will be given to him" (James 1:5). When James says, "If you lack wisdom," he is not suggesting that some people have it all together and some don't. He is letting us know that everyone lacks God's wisdom. However, not everyone recognizes his or her need.

To obtain God's wisdom, you must endure trials joyfully, acknowledge your need, and trust God to meet it. I never would have seen the change in my life if I had not finally become honest with myself. I had to acknowledge that I had failed so many times and hurt so many people. Yes, it hurt, but it was those times of confession and repentance that gave me the strength to rise up and be the woman God had purposed me to be.

RENEW YOUR MIND

In part, renewing your mind means fumigating old, dead things so you can live free of oppression, depression, and mind control. First you must admit that you have allowed the things of this world—people, places, and things—to dominate you. You have to make up your mind that you are ready for change. Then God will lead you by His Word and His Spirit into greater and greater levels of freedom.

Let's take another look at Philippians chapter 4, this time from the New International Version.

> Finally, brothers, whatever is true, whatever is noble, whatever is right, whatever is pure, whatever is lovely, whatever is admirable, if anything is excellent or praiseworthy, think about such things. Whatever you have learned or received or heard from me, or seen in me, put it into practice. And the God of peace will be with you.
> —PHILIPPIANS 4:8–9, NIV

This is an excellent passage to memorize and use for direction in life. Paul tells us to think only about things that are true, noble, right, pure, lovely, admirable, excellent, or praiseworthy. It tells us what we should be thinking about and implies thousands of things we should not. If we take this instruction to heart, peace will overtake us.

Would you be at peace if you were imprisoned and facing a death sentence, as Paul was? You could be! Paul received a key that unlocked the power God promised to Him. He allowed God's truth to be his filter, which means he had a standard that distinguished his own truth (his circumstances, attitudes, etc.) from God's pure truth. Paul had to clean out any destructive thoughts, habits, and decisions that could have led him away from God. In other words, he had to fumigate.

If you want your life to change, fumigation is critical. There can be no real or lasting change without it. Yet there is more, and Paul gave us clues in his letter to the Ephesians:

> Put off, concerning your former conduct, the old man which grows corrupt according to the deceitful lusts, and be renewed in the spirit of your mind, and that you put on the new man which was created according to God, in true righteousness and holiness.
>
> —EPHESIANS 4:22–24

Three things jump out at me from this passage, and renewing the mind is sandwiched right in the middle of them.

Put off the old man and his old ways.

You cannot find your true passion, the love for life, and the peace that surpasses all understanding until you allow the Holy Spirit to assist you in dumping the influences that have held you hostage. The old man of the flesh is full of lusts and confusion. Therefore, he cannot consistently make positive decisions.

You can decide today that your past conduct cannot camp out in your present or follow you into your future.

Be renewed in your mind.

We have already seen that we become what we think about most of the time. What negativity is preoccupying you? Are you thinking about failed relationships, lost jobs, not enough income, rebellious children, or an adulterous spouse? You are no doubt dealing with some negative situations. However, you can set your mind on the Word of God and watch Him begin a new work in you.

You cannot renew your mind by continually doing the things that caused you to be imprisoned in the first place. It makes no logical sense to believe that will work. To receive what you have never had, you must do things you have never done.

Reality television and social media might seem enjoyable, but they are not helping you move forward. Are you shocked that I listed social media, knowing that my pulpit ministry began from my online outreach?

I am not condemning social media; I am suggesting that your focus needs to change. It is important for everyone to take a break and spend quality time with God. Even I realize that my quiet time in the presence of the Lord is what prepares me to travel and face all sorts of demons while God releases thousands of people from destruction.

Put on the new man.

Putting on the new man does not mean shedding your skin and becoming a brand-new person from the outside in. That just does not work. However, if you become brand-new on the inside, your inside will dominate your outside. When your thinking changes, your emotions (which are dominated by what you think about most) also change. And because your emotions determine your actions, your actions change too.

When you put off the old man of flesh, renew your mind, and put on the new man, everyone will see a new you.

YOUR PLACE IN THE BODY

Paul instructs us to live in ways that reflect our new values. When we do, we can fulfill God's plan for us. That's not just a personal thing; it is also a "body of Christ" thing.

Your body is made up of many organs. Though most of them are hidden from sight, you cannot function without them. Often the most important organs are the ones you cannot see. Think what happens when your heartbeat is irregular. It can cause the release of blood clots that could take your life in a moment!

When God formed you in your mother's womb, He established the importance of each body part. That's why I spend time naming and praying for each part of my body. I ask God to keep my organs working as He designed them to work—to release toxins, allow oxygen to flow through my circulatory system, and keep my heartbeat steady.

Why am I saying this? It's because it parallels how God sees Christ's body in the earth. You are an important part of His body. You might not be speaking to thousands of people each week, but if you are loving your family, neighbors, or fellow employees, you are vital to the kingdom of God.

As you experience regeneration in Christ, you naturally desire to be a viable member of His body. Even before Christ, God's servants sensed their places in God's larger kingdom. Joseph saw God's plan for his life revealed in two dreams. The road to his destiny was anything but easy. His brothers sold him into slavery in Egypt. He was later sent to prison, even though he was innocent of any crime. Years later Joseph was released from prison to become second in command to Pharaoh.

That was his destiny! God knew a terrible famine would come while Joseph was in power. His presence in Egypt meant that his own family (the nation of Israel) would survive the famine.

After he saved them, Joseph's brothers were afraid that when their father, Jacob, passed away, Joseph would retaliate against them. Joseph's response revealed a renewed mind in action:

> "But as for you, you meant evil against me; but God meant it for good, in order to bring it about as it is this day, to save many people alive. Now therefore, do not be afraid; I will provide for you and

your little ones." And he comforted them and spoke
kindly to them.

—Genesis 50:20–21

Joseph did not allow bitterness to determine his actions,
but he did let his brothers know how God turned their
wicked plans around for good. Because he understood God's
will and his own place in it, Joseph helped to ensure Israel's
destiny in God.

You can do the same, allowing God to make you a new
man or woman in Christ, day by day.

KEEP DISTRACTIONS IN CHECK

As you filter the thoughts that invade your mind, you realize
that carnal thoughts harass you without your active permission. It can happen when your pastor is preaching about steps
to a victorious life, and your mind drifts to a certain movie
scene or a bill that needs to be paid. Maybe you awaken in
the middle of the night to revisit a failed relationship or a
lost job that is troubling you.

Even when you try to focus on good things, negative
scenes play out in your mind. I am happy to tell you that
God has a strategy to win the battles that want to overtake
your mind. It is a scripture we last talked about in chapter 8,
and it is a great one to memorize.

God's Word says that we overcome by "casting down
arguments and every high thing that exalts itself against the
knowledge of God, bringing every thought into captivity to
the obedience of Christ" (2 Cor. 10:5). I cannot tell you how
many times a week I use this verse to frame my reality. I
speak to myself continually, casting down ideas that try to
rule me negatively. I sometimes even lay hands on my head
as I cast down anything that tries to rob me of the peace
that God gives.

This is so important because the world is full of cares, and we have more obligations than we can meet by ourselves. However, we can bring every doubt and fear into captivity by being obedient to Christ and by feeding ourselves on Him.

This is how we change from the inside out. When we feed on the right "food" and cast down the junk, we can see life through brand-new filters. "Therefore, holy brothers and sisters, who share in the heavenly calling, fix your thoughts on Jesus, whom we acknowledge as our apostle and high priest" (Heb. 3:1, NIV).

I remember driving a car that looked like a Bentley but overheated and stranded me daily. It sat in the shop often. My parents and I spent thousands to fix it. But nothing worked. It was a beautiful jalopy!

We sometimes face problems that go on and on like that jalopy. Whatever the issue is, we need to fix our thoughts on Jesus and not the distractions. My car was a huge distraction, but I could not blame anyone else. I had to ask Jesus for forgiveness and then forgive myself (more on that in a minute). However, as I sat on the side of the road, I could not let my joy be stolen. I had found freedom from the inside out, and it was affecting my external condition. The car had not changed. Neither had the one-hour commute and the daily breakdowns. Yet I decided that the situation would not take me out.

My faith was on the right track, but I needed more spiritual nourishment and fumigating. After I moved back into my parents' house, I knew I had to turn in the leased luxury cars. However, my flesh was not yet crucified, and I still wanted those kinds of cars. I really wanted an automobile that looked like a Bentley. So I asked my dad to help me find one. After all the pain I'd been through, he wanted to give me any happiness he could. He did his best to pick out a car, but shortly after I got it, the car started acting up. For years we kept repairing it.

Eventually I realized that I could not call my dad every time the car broke down. I started traveling with a large jug of water and an antifreeze mixture. When the car overheated, I poured the mixture into the radiator and waited.

Who knew that this humiliating season would be followed by a platform on social media? I could have allowed my troubles to rob me of the future joy of loving friends around the world back to life, both online and in the pulpit. However, instead I learned to fix my thoughts on Jesus, and He worked everything out for my good.

I remember a saying my mom often quoted: "Your actions speak so loud, I can't hear what you're saying." To become mature Christians, we must balance and discipline our thoughts and emotions. We may have used coping skills to protect us from our hurts and pains in the past, but now those skills can keep us from living in reality.

For your life to be changed today, you must work with God. Take a moment to inventory your thoughts and actions. Determine that you will not allow your feelings to take you on a detrimental path. Fumigate your thinking and renew your mind. You have the tools. Now use them.

Jesus, I realize that it's up to me to let You change my life. I surrender and ask You to take over. Cleanse my mind and become Lord of my life. Give me fortitude to make the right decisions for total healing.

I DECLARE

I decree and declare that I am a new creation in Christ Jesus. Old things are passed away, and I am walking in the newness of life.

CHAPTER 11

THE IN-BETWEEN

THROUGHOUT OUR JOURNEY together we have discussed areas that you are determined to change. To make those changes, you need direction and faith to believe the adjustments will lead to something positive. You also need to understand that change involves transitions, or in-between places. Transition can make you uneasy and even afraid, which can prompt poor decisions that leave you "paralyzed" and unable to act.

For example, you may be on a weight-loss journey, wondering whether you will ever reach your goal. You change your lifestyle and even your friends. You do whatever is necessary to achieve your ideal weight, yet progress is much slower than you expected. You refuse to purchase new clothes until you are where you need to be. You keep cinching your belt, hoping to keep your current wardrobe until you can totally replace it. Then one day your pants practically fall down, and you realize it's time to buy some new clothes.

The in-between stage of losing weight is uncomfortable. Besides concerns about what to wear, you might fear losing weight and gaining it back again. So you keep a closet full of larger sizes, just in case.

The transition that comes after a divorce or the death of a spouse can have similar effects. When you are between stages, it is hard to find where you belong. You are used to being part of a twosome. You were so comfortable and secure in the relationship. All your friends knew you as part of a pair. Now you must find a new scene and a new lifestyle. It's not easy, but you have to do it.

The same is true after you graduate from college and are looking for a job that fits. Discovering your place in the world can be challenging and even awkward. Yet finding your way is completely necessary. Until you navigate your transition, you cannot enter the next season of your life.

I call the in-between stage *the waiting season*. When you are in it, you will be tempted to back away. But don't give in to the temptation. Exercise your faith. Remind yourself that a new season is on the horizon and you can do this!

THE WAITING SEASON

The challenge with waiting seasons is that we live in a right-now society. We want our weight loss now, our new job now, our new house now. It can be difficult to stay in peace when the in-between time takes longer than expected.

GOD IS WORKING ON THAT THING YOU'RE WORRYING ABOUT; TAKE YOUR HANDS OFF THE WHEEL!
—*@RealTalkKim*

I have learned that God does not live in my time. He lives in eternity, and His schedule is much different from mine. I can pray about wanting and needing patience; however, I have learned to just live my life. Everyday trials develop in me all the patience I need, *if* I allow the process.

My dad often told a story about a woman at a revival where he was ministering who came to the altar crying out for patience. As the pastors prayed over her, they asked the Lord to send her tribulation, because the Bible says that tribulations brings perseverance, or patience. The woman cried out, "Oh no, I don't need any more trials. I have enough to worry about now."

This story taught me not to ask for patience! Yet even without asking for it, my patience has grown exponentially because of poor decisions that brought many cares and tribulations. I have learned to allow the Holy Spirit to mold me through these experiences so I can become a new vessel for His purpose.

Early in my process of transformation, I expected change to happen immediately. However, when I decided that I was ready for change, I discovered that change wasn't ready for me. My mind, will, and emotions were not yet in a place that would allow me to become the patient mother, loving daughter, and all-around good friend I wanted to be.

Change doesn't happen the same day we decide we want it. And it rarely happens the way we think it should. It is a matter of seeing through a different lens and hearing through different ears. It reminds me of what happens when you tell the same story to several people. If you listen as they repeat it to others, you'll hear a slightly different story each time. That is because we are different and we hear through different grids.

Because I was so independent and always believed I was right, I had a difficult time allowing others to give me direction. I thought I understood life and needed no one to guide me. Now I wonder how I got to the place where no one could tell me anything. I know I didn't get there overnight. Everything I heard had to pass through my grid, and I did not realize I was resisting whatever challenged my mind-set.

When I moved back to my parents' home, my dad realized how fragile I had become. He told my mom it would take at least a year for me to heal and gain victory. He had no idea that it would be three years before I would begin to really listen to God and allow Him to work His process through me.

That was when I knew I was on a journey toward freedom, and that knowledge released an excitement in me that I had never experienced. Each day I looked forward to spending time with the Lord. I hungered for His Word. I had never spent time in His Word before, so this was a brand-new experience.

ACTIVE WAITING AND MATURITY

By now it probably comes as no surprise to you that I was a preacher's kid who knew very little about what the Bible actually said. I cannot explain how I sat on the church pew with my mother each week, was involved in all the youth activities, and sang in the choir, yet ended up like someone who had never been in church.

Looking back, I can see that my grid kept me distracted. I was so busy judging and criticizing others that I never allowed the Holy Spirit to fill me. I sang on worship teams and watched the Holy Spirit move through congregations. But I never opened the door to my heart, surrendered myself totally, or welcomed Him in. It was as though I had been unchurched my entire life.

I was simply not mature in Christ—not on any level. I did not know how to actively wait, so I was not changing. Becoming a mature believer means understanding God's position in your life and realizing that He is not some kind of Santa Claus who makes your life easy just because you decide to call on Him. Many Bible stories are about people who struggled for years yet stayed in faith, believing that God would see them through. In Hebrews 11, the "honor roll" of faith, many faithful warriors died before God fulfilled His promise to them. Yet they died believing it would come.

As we mature, we realize that God's promises are eternal. They are not about cars, houses, clothes, or diamonds. They are about eternity and the assurance of spending it with God. Each of our lives is like a dot on a page, but eternity is like a line that goes on forever. When we are young, we think we have so much time to accomplish everything we want to do that we spend our days frivolously. We play around, believing we'll get to make up for whatever we missed. Yet it seems as though we turn around and find ourselves middle-aged.

I can tell you that I wasted eighteen years thinking I had plenty of time. Therefore, I had no motivation to hear what the Father was saying. When I awakened to my situation at thirty-six years of age, my boys were broken, and we were a distraught, hopeless family. That was when I knew I had to get my act together.

I am so thankful that God gave me another chance to break out of my complacency and selfishness. Life is much shorter than I could have imagined, but He graciously granted me time to set things right.

ONE DAY EVERYTHING THAT BROKE YOU
GOD WILL USE TO RESTORE YOU.
MY GOD IS A MIRACLE WORKER!
—@RealTalkKim

LEARNING TO WAIT

In Philippians 4:11 Paul wrote, "Not that I speak in regard to need, for I have learned in whatever state I am, to be content." Discontentment is such a driver in our society. People seem to move from one goal to the next, searching for something that will satisfy them or cause others to be in awe of them.

Everyone is trying to find contentment and peace, even if just for a season. So much of our activity is a substitute for what we were created to do, which is to wait for God to fulfill His promises. It happens in the church as well as the secular world. Many people in church are so caught up with looking for the next great church or the next big revival that they cannot lay their heads down at night without being buzzed out of their spiritual consciousness. They have no idea how to be at peace where God has placed them. If the spotlight is not shining on them, they are trying to understand their purpose, their plan. They don't realize that God has a searchlight that can expose every area of pain while bringing wholeness; however, each one of us must allow Him to search our hearts. That is something we do privately with God; it cannot be done publicly.

I cannot describe the loneliness I felt as I walked out my journey of healing with no one but the Lord. It was my time of letting go of everyone who had assisted in creating the chaos that had become as normal as breathing. I had to learn how to stop the roller coaster of life and just sit by a cool stream emotionally while allowing God to root out and dig up all the negatives that had become my way of life.

Depression medication and sleeping pills cannot bring the contentment Paul talked about in Philippians 4. Contentment comes at a price: we have to come to the end of ourselves and realize that material things cannot make us happy. When we learn to accept life's blessings without comparing ourselves with others, we open ourselves to a whole new kind of living.

Our society sets false values on every level. One value says that more is better. We are into designer labels, specialty cars, and the latest gadgets. I am not judging those who like to play around with new technology and use certain brands. I too like the latest gadgets and labels. However, I know they cannot provide contentment. They are just things, and things pass away. They cannot help us in our darkest times, and they cannot eliminate the waiting season that prepares us for what is next.

So how do we endure the waiting period that stands between right now and the fulfillment of God's promises of restoration? It is amazing how often I hear people wanting someone to pray instant abundance into their lives. We are always in a hurry, but God often seems to take His time. He lives in eternity, after all. His perspective of time is different from ours. Yet no matter how long He seems to take, we can know that He has a plan and purpose for every choice He makes. With God the waiting time is never a waste of time.

> The Lord is not slack concerning His promise, as some count slackness, but is longsuffering toward us, not willing that any should perish but that all should come to repentance.
>
> —2 PETER 3:9

The Lord does not delay His promises, as we understand delay. He is patient with us, not wanting any of us to perish or become entangled in things we are unprepared to handle.

WITH GOD THE WAITING TIME IS NEVER A WASTE OF TIME.
—@RealTalkKim

Whether we realize it or not, we are always waiting. In fact, much of life seems to be all about waiting. I don't know about you, but when I go to a doctor's appointment, I get agitated knowing I could be waiting an hour to be seen, even though I arrived on time. When I dial a company's automated phone system, I am not thrilled about having to answer so many questions and press so many buttons before I get to talk to a human being about my situation.

Because we live in a right-now society, our blood pressure increases and we become frustrated when we have to wait. But waiting is an important part of maturing in Christ. Waiting does not mean stopping everything until God says, "Go." As I once read a pastor say, "Those who wait are those who work, because they know their work is not in vain. The farmer can wait all summer for his harvest because he has done his work of sowing the seed and watering the plants."[1]

The people named in Hebrews chapter 11 were like the farmer who works and waits, knowing the cause is worthwhile. They kept "plowing" even though the ultimate harvest did not come in their lifetimes. The writer of Hebrews mentions Noah, Abraham, Sarah, Jacob, Moses, and others. "These all died in faith, not having received the promises, but having seen them afar off were assured of them, embraced them and confessed that they were strangers and pilgrims on the earth" (Heb. 11:13).

Their testimonies remind us that we are going somewhere. If we remain faithful and obedient, as they did, no matter how long it takes, we will receive what God promised.

WAITING HAS ITS REWARDS

Do you know the story of Jesus and His friends Lazarus, Mary, and Martha? Because they were such close friends, Mary and Martha contacted Jesus immediately after their brother, Lazarus, became ill. They knew Jesus was a miracle worker, and they believed He could heal their brother. However, when Jesus heard that Lazarus was sick, He did not rush to his side. He said, "This sickness is not unto death, but for the glory of God, that the Son of God may be glorified through it" (John 11:4).

By the time Jesus arrived at His friends' home in Bethany (just two miles from Jerusalem), Lazarus had been buried for four days. Martha told Jesus that her brother would still be alive if Jesus had come sooner.

Jesus had a different perspective. He did not see death as Mary and Martha saw it. He knew how the story would end. When He called His dead friend out of the tomb, Lazarus emerged alive. Everyone watched in amazement, and the Bible says, "Then many of the Jews who had come to Mary, and had seen the things Jesus did, believed in Him" (John 11:45). With their brother resurrected and so many coming to believe in Jesus, Mary and Martha began to understand what it meant to be content with waiting.

How many times have you been upset because your prayers were not answered when you first prayed? Does Lazarus' story help you to see how perfect God's timing is? The next time you are ready for transformation but see no evidence of it, you don't have to lose heart. God knows the end of the story before it even begins, and He knows where you are going!

YOU MAY BE TIRED, DISCOURAGED, AND FRUSTRATED, BUT DON'T GIVE UP. YOUR SITUATION IS ABOUT TO CHANGE!
—*@RealTalkKim*

In a million years I could never have dreamed that God would open the world to me. I could not have planned my unexpected journey because I live only in the present time. God is the One who lives in eternity. When I step onto a platform today and see thousands of hungry faces ready to receive what I have come to give, I am still shocked that God is using me. I pinch myself several times a day as invitations come in to minister at large churches. I even question why they would want me to preach when there are so many great speakers available.

I could not have known where my waiting would lead. It was not for me to determine my path but only to follow God's direction. Psalm 37:23 tells me that the steps of a good man or woman are ordered by the Lord. I just need to stay in His presence and wait on Him as He does His work.

Remember that Paul said you can be content in any state or condition, just as you can walk in great favor and still have problems. Contentment is essential in your waiting seasons, and it comes by faith.

Choosing contentment will be disruptive if your status quo is to be dissatisfied. Accessing where you are going often means disrupting where you are.

I believe my story is a modern-day example of someone having to experience a dry, dark place with more questions than answers before learning how to thrive. So many people tell me that they listen to my messages because they know I passed the pain test. That is human nature: we want to hear from those who have made it through the struggle. It gives us the faith to keep going when the going is really tough.

You cannot teach others how to make it until you endure the process yourself and pass the test. If you choose to keep going, your pain will produce an anointing that will empower you to help others find victory.

THE POWER OF PATIENCE

What if instead of repairing your past and restoring what was lost, God wanted to give you something you never had in the first place?

I love the verse that says, "Behold, I will do a new thing, now it shall spring forth; shall you not know it? I will even make a road in the wilderness and rivers in the desert" (Isa. 43:19).

No matter how broken you feel today, God can bring you to the expected end He purposed long before you were born.

It is not a matter of how long you wait but of *how you wait*. Most people struggle with waiting, especially when it means a long-term commitment. They are seeking short-term gains. In writing to the Philippians, Paul expressed his heart, the heart of a man who had peace and patience knowing he was about to die. Paul learned to be content in difficult times because His commitment reached into eternity.

That made Paul willing to delay his gratification. Really, that is the essence of patience. If you cannot wait for God, you cannot see His blessings. If you cannot trust Him to do the small things, you will never see exploits in the spiritual realm. Do you want to see your family put back together? Do you long to sleep a full night without nightmares? Do you want to pay your bills without borrowing? Do you need a friend who will be there when you call?

IT IS NOT A MATTER OF HOW LONG YOU WAIT
BUT OF HOW YOU WAIT.
—@RealTalkKim

"Be anxious for nothing, but in everything by prayer and supplication, with thanksgiving, let your requests be made known to God" (Phil. 4:6). I realize that I have quoted this verse often. However, it keeps me focused on prayer because Paul says that instead of worrying, we are to pray about everything.

When you develop the habit of praying instead of being anxious or complaining, your attitude toward everything changes. Expectation (the strong belief that something *will* happen) becomes a natural part of living because you are actively standing in faith. You will always be on the edge of your seat, waiting for the "next scene" to unfold and experiencing the amazing feelings you get right before your expectation becomes a reality.

While my boys and I lived with my parents, we could not picture our lives being any different. I knew we could not afford anything more than what we had. It was a difficult season, and I felt like a failure. But when God began to show me what was ahead in the spiritual realm, my focus shifted. I knew we wouldn't live with "less than" or never have enough. I became thankful for every opportunity to prove God's promises. I began to believe that He would restore all that I had lost and give me restitution for all that the enemy had stolen from my family.

The Lord assured me that He was my provider. Even when my husband, Mark, and I were married six years ago, we were starting over. Just moving into a leased home was exciting because our family was together. There are no words to describe how we felt when we actually purchased a home. I never dreamed I would be able to borrow money again because I had lost my business and my credit was ruined. Six years after I lost my business, I assumed my credit was still damaged. I did not realize that even though my dad had cosigned my automobile loan, I was rebuilding my credit with each payment.

Even when you can't see that God is working, He is working all things for your good. (See Romans 8:28.) My family and I have seen it firsthand! We waited for our blessings to be revealed, and God blessed us beyond our wildest dreams. We continually give God thanks for all He has done for us.

I had to exercise patience in every area where change was needed. I cannot tell you how different I am from the full-of-demands, impatient-with-everyone person I used to be. Today I can see how God allowed my persecutions and trials to mold me into a person of character who strives to please Him while loving other people back to life. He developed my character as I invited Him to do His best work through me. It started when I admitted that I could no longer do it myself. The process changed me from a selfish, hard-hearted, self-protecting person to an amazing child of God who lives life to the fullest, out on the edge. Now my whole life's desire is to love others while serving God.

Even Abraham had to learn patience. Scripture says that after he "patiently endured, he obtained the promise" (Heb. 6:15). In other words, Abraham waited. Waiting transforms people who once conformed to the ways of the world and turns them into people who live to please God. While we wait on the promises God gives us, we grow in our ability to depend on Him and trust Him completely to do what we cannot.

Many of the great men and women in Scripture had something in common: they knew their victories resulted from their dependency on God.[2] That dependency takes time to develop. I recently read that "when God wants to grow mushrooms, he can do it overnight, but when he wants to grow a mighty oak, it takes a few years. What do we want to be, a mushroom or an oak? If we want to be an oak, it is well worth the wait."[3]

To become a disciplined follower of Christ who does great exploits, you have to go through the waiting season. You *will* experience highs and lows. At times you will have less than what you need, and at other times you will be blessed abundantly. These circumstances do not define your strength. Your strength is determined by how well you (1) stay connected to your purpose and (2) understand that God is your strength.

IF YOU CANNOT CONTROL SELF, SELF WILL CONTROL YOU.
—@RealTalkKim

Being disciplined is an important aspect of patience. Having discipline means having a conscious say over your lifestyle. I truly believe that a lack of discipline results from a lack of intimacy with God. Scripture confirms this by saying that "the fruit of the Spirit is love, joy, peace, long-suffering, kindness, goodness, faithfulness, gentleness, *self-control*. Against such there is no law" (Gal. 5:22–23).

God did not create us to be disobedient or lacking in self-control. He gave us the fruit of the Spirit to help us. If you cannot control self, self will control you. The values of a disciplined person are evident in his spiritual life and in everything he does for the Lord. Disciplined people are typically known as people of character. When their discipline is godly, it is because they are led by the Holy Spirit. To become the giant slayer you want to be, you must be led by the Holy Spirit rather than your feelings. Feelings can lie to you, but God's Word and Spirit are true.

Our goal is to be like Jesus. As long as we keep our focus on the Lord, we will be able to stand firm in faith, even in our in-between seasons, knowing that He is working behind the scenes. As we near the end of our journey together, let's acknowledge that a growth process has begun inside. We have decided to follow Jesus, and there is no turning back. Our trajectories are shifting us from where we are to where He is leading us—and we are ready!

> *Lord Jesus, I respond to Your call to be the vessel You purposed me to be in Psalm 139. I am ready for change and will allow the Holy Spirit to mold and make me into a vessel of transformation. Amen.*

I DECLARE

I decree and declare that I am called by God to change my world. I will arise daily, surrender my desire for control, and allow God to take over. God, I give You permission to rule and reign over my spirit, soul, and body as I do Your will today.

CHAPTER 12

WE SEE A MESS; GOD SEES A CHANCE!

THE OBSTACLES IN your life are God's opportunities to reveal Himself to you. He turns your mess into a message and your test into your testimony. God never wastes a hurt. Psalm 56:8 says, "You keep track of all my sorrows. You have collected all my tears in your bottle. You have recorded each one in your book" (NLT). God is sensitive to your pain and desires your wholeness. Your wound might not be your fault, but your healing is your responsibility. What you deem as failure God uses to promote you into your next season.

When David wrote Psalm 56, he was held captive by the Philistines and knew that only God would be his strength. He trusted God, knowing He understood every sorrow and fear and would take care of him, no matter how deep his despair was. I'm not sure how David saw his tears being collected in a bottle, but those tears resulted from pain, so his insight was very personal. David could not help sharing how God made sure none of his tears went to waste. We talk about accepting Jesus as our personal Savior; what an example David was of having a personal relationship with God!

God loves us intensely. In Ephesians 5:2 Paul said that Jesus' death on the cross was a fragrant offering and sacrifice to God. I am amazed that our heavenly Father gave His only begotten Son to walk this earth as a sacrifice, to be our pattern in life, and to die in our stead. I don't know how I could have lived so many years in selfishness, not even considering what Jesus Christ did for me. My only consolation is knowing that when God saw the mess my life had become, He also saw a chance to make it amazing.

GOD IS NOT PUNISHING YOU; HE'S PREPARING YOU.
TRUST HIS PLAN, NOT YOUR PAIN.
—*@RealTalkKim*

FROM SAUL TO PAUL

A prime example of how God turns a mess into a message is the life of Saul of Tarsus, who fiercely persecuted Christians. Saul was born into a family from the strictest sect of Judaism, and he was educated under the great rabbi Gamaliel. Saul was known as a Pharisee of Pharisees, who eagerly hunted down the followers of Jesus. After becoming Paul, he explained his history to the church at Galatia:

> You have heard of my former conduct in Judaism, how I persecuted the church of God beyond measure and tried to destroy it. And I advanced in Judaism beyond many of my contemporaries in my own nation, being more exceedingly zealous for the traditions of my fathers.
>
> —GALATIANS 1:13–14

Saul was a great threat and saw murdering Christians as a great honor. Therefore, he sought permission to arrest Christians in Damascus and bring them to Jerusalem to be punished or even killed.

Then Saul, still breathing threats and murder against the disciples of the Lord, went to the high priest and asked letters from him to the synagogues of Damascus, so that if he found any who were of the Way, whether men or women, he might bring them bound to Jerusalem.

—Acts 9:1–2

Saul got the permission he wanted and headed to Damascus. His trip was interrupted by an encounter with Christ.

As he journeyed he came near Damascus, and suddenly a light shone around him from heaven. Then he fell to the ground, and heard a voice saying to him, "Saul, Saul, why are you persecuting Me?" And he said, "Who are You, Lord?" Then the Lord said, "I am Jesus, whom you are persecuting. It is hard for you to kick against the goads."

So he, trembling and astonished, said, "Lord, what do You want me to do?" Then the Lord said to him, "Arise and go into the city, and you will be told what you must do." And the men who journeyed with him stood speechless, hearing a voice but seeing no one. Then Saul arose from the ground, and when his eyes were opened he saw no one. But they led him by the hand and brought him into Damascus. And he was three days without sight, and neither ate nor drank.

—Acts 9:3–9

Can you imagine what the men traveling with Saul were thinking when they saw no one but heard a voice booming from out of nowhere? I think I would have become a believer

157

immediately! Because Saul recognized that the voice was God's, he immediately obeyed the instructions and went into the city and waited for further instructions.

Since he had been struck blind, those traveling with him led him into the city. When he arrived there, Saul received a visit from Ananias of Damascus, whom God had instructed to lay hands on Saul to restore his sight. Of course, Ananias was reluctant to obey because he knew Saul as a man who was trying to destroy the followers of Christ. However, Ananias followed the orders God had given him. He prayed for Saul, baptized him, and saw him filled with the Holy Spirit.

Saul's conversion turned his life upside down! Even his name was changed. The man who thought he was doing God a favor by killing Christians no longer wanted to hurt anyone. Instead, he became the greatest evangelist of his day and eventually wrote over half the New Testament. He listened to God and believed that even a religious, domineering man like himself could be called by God to change his world. Paul had only to get out of God's way.

Anyone whose life has been turned upside down by a life change can probably relate to Paul's story. I know I can. Is God telling you it's time to get out of His way? Are you praying fear-based prayers because the enemy accused you of causing your own wounds? God will forgive you, even if you had a hand in your suffering. Paul could have found every imaginable excuse to be disqualified by God and forsake His instructions. Yet he yielded, took responsibility for his sins, and accepted God's forgiveness.

PREPARE TO MOVE FORWARD

For God to elevate you to your next level sometimes requires separation from the things that have kept you stuck. It can be your busy lifestyle that puts everything before God. Even your friends may influence you to look in every direction before you seek God's will. After his conversion Paul could have allowed doubt and fear to distract him from God's will. The fear of what others would think could easily have defined his direction. He could have gone straight to Jerusalem to learn from the apostles who had walked with Jesus and to seek their approval. He could also have gotten ahead of God by immediately building a ministry platform, traveling, and sharing his testimony.

Paul did none of those things. Instead, he spent three years in Arabia, realizing that he needed to separate himself even from religious circles. Galatians 1:12 suggests that Paul spent that time studying the teachings of Christ. His time was obviously fruitful because when Paul went to Jerusalem fourteen years after his conversion and met privately with church leaders, they found that "there was absolutely no difference between what he had been teaching for eleven years in Antioch and what the apostles had been teaching in Jerusalem, Judea, and Samaria."[1]

Paul did not allow his past to determine his future. He released himself from the guilt of his cruelty to others. He walked in forgiveness, even forgiving himself. He also allowed the Lord Jesus to instruct and prepare him for his next season.

I doubt the devil was happy about Paul's conversion and ministry. Scripture tells us to be "strong and courageous. Do not be afraid; do not be discouraged, for the Lord your God will be with you wherever you go" (Josh. 1:9, NIV). I said this earlier: The enemy can see who you are, even in your premature state. He is not trying to kill you. He is trying to kill the deliverer in you. He is not after who you are but who you are going to be.

If I had known at eighteen about the international call on my life, I might not have created the storms that kept me in crisis. I had no idea that my decisions at eighteen would hinder my life for another eighteen years. Yet God knew every decision I would make before I made it, and still He decided to be there when I called.

If you knew what God purposed when He wrote your name in His book, you would disconnect from people who are trying to steal your dreams. Scripture says, "Your eyes saw my substance, being yet unformed. And in Your book, they all were written, the days fashioned for me, when as yet there were none of them" (Ps. 139:16). When you discover that you have been chosen by God to fulfill a purpose, you know you have to make decisions for your future. Paul's decision for Christ changed everything. Before that he was revered by the Jews as one of the most learned men of his day. After that he spread the gospel everywhere he went.

The fact that you're reading this book tells me you are ready for change. That change comes at a cost. Among other things, it means letting go of people who refuse to embrace your growth and entrance into your next chapter. You cannot take your excess baggage into your calling. The writer of Hebrews wrote, "Since we are surrounded by so great a cloud of witnesses, let us lay aside every weight, and the sin which so easily ensnares us, and let us run with endurance the race that is set before us" (Heb. 12:1).

A *weight* is anything that keeps you from moving forward. Just because God showed you your destiny does not mean it will come to pass. You have to cooperate with God. I have seen overweight people complain about their health but refuse to change their lifestyles. You cannot complain about poor health and eat fast food every day. Don't ask me to pray for your cholesterol level to go down when you refuse to change your diet, even after your physician warned you of the consequences of maintaining unhealthy habits.

I have seen many people's prophetic words go unfulfilled

because they lacked character or were too lazy to pursue God and begin to walk out the plans He spoke through those words. I have learned in my journey that God does not answer your list of wants with a bagful of goodies. He took time to give you unique attributes, gifts, and abilities for His own good pleasure and yours. However, you have to prepare yourself to use them.

YOU CANNOT TAKE YOUR EXCESS BAGGAGE INTO YOUR CALLING.
—@RealTalkKim

When you don't get the promotion, ask yourself why not. Is it because of race or gender bias, or because you were not prepared for your next level? Some people want to be leaders in their churches but have no idea how to be faithful attendees.

Lots of traits can keep promotion and elevation out of your reach. Let's examine a few of them.

Disobedience

One dictionary defines *disobedience* as "failure or refusal to obey rules or someone in authority."[2] Another source says, "To be disobedient is to yield to self-will instead of surrendering to God and desiring His will in all things."[3] These definitions apply in the natural and the spiritual. When you know the rules but don't follow them, you negate your opportunities for elevation. As one Bible teacher wrote, "God expects obedience," which "is the practical acceptance of the authority and will of God."[4] That includes your response to those who have leadership over you.

You could say that the first law of elevation is to obey rules and laws. It is certainly true in biblical terms.

> This Book of the Law shall not depart from your
> mouth, but you shall meditate in it day and night,

that you may observe to do according to all that is written in it. For then you will make your way prosperous, and then you will have good success.

—Joshua 1:8

This amazing promise is also an instruction to meditate on (or study) God's Word. That is how we walk by faith and not by sight. We expect God to open doors for us, give us new jobs, and help us become successful. However, we have to do our part.

How many times has your pastor given you a word from the Lord on Sunday, yet you failed to apply it throughout the week? Just hearing the Word does not improve your opportunities for advancement. You have to *do* what the Word says to realize the promised benefit.

Jonah 1:2–3 says:

"Arise, go to Nineveh, that great city, and cry out against it; for their wickedness has come up before Me." But Jonah arose to flee to Tarshish from the presence of the Lord. He went down to Joppa, and found a ship going to Tarshish; so he paid the fare, and went down into it, to go with them to Tarshish from the presence of the Lord.

Jonah was swallowed by a big fish because he rejected God's instruction to go to Nineveh and bought a ticket to Joppa instead. God didn't abandon Jonah for rejecting Him. He provided a very special mode of transportation to help motivate Jonah. Then He waited for Jonah to obey. Jonah was a mess, but God saw a chance for him to excel.

We sometimes try to design plans we think are "safer" or more practical than God's instructions. That is what King Saul did when the prophet Samuel instructed him to destroy the spoils of his victory over the Amalekites and kill the defeated king.

> Saul attacked the Amalekites, from Havilah all the way to Shur, which is east of Egypt. He also took Agag king of the Amalekites alive, and utterly destroyed all the people with the edge of the sword. But Saul and the people spared Agag and the best of the sheep, the oxen, the fatlings, the lambs, and all that was good, and were unwilling to utterly destroy them. But everything despised and worthless, that they utterly destroyed.
>
> —1 SAMUEL 15:7–9

Saul destroyed the people and the worst of the flocks, but he spared King Agag and the best animals. Because he disobeyed God, God rejected Saul as king and elevated David. Being partially obedient is not good enough for God. In fact, it's sin. This seems obvious when we read about people like Saul. Yet we can be oblivious to our own disobedience.

Sometimes we fail to advance because we have not fully complied with what God has already instructed. He has given us His Word, but we have to choose our direction. It is easy to hear the truth every Sunday and change absolutely nothing. We might choose to keep a live-in partner or refuse to curb our emotional spending. We live in such confusion that we cannot make simple decisions. It is not that God is failing us but that we are failing Him and ourselves.

Don't you know that God sees every bit of your future? He has a plan for you. He said so Himself!

> I know the thoughts that I think toward you, says the LORD, thoughts of peace and not of evil, to give you a future and a hope. Then you will call upon

Me and go and pray to Me, and I will listen to
you. And you will seek Me and find Me, when you
search for Me with all your heart.
—JEREMIAH 29:11–13

God gave us this powerful promise in Jeremiah 29:11, and
some of us quote it all the time. But do we forget about verses
12 and 13? God tells us to seek Him with all our hearts and
then we will find Him. Our misunderstandings of obedience
and our hesitations might seem minor, yet they cause significant damage. For you to even understand God's purpose in
your life requires obedience to His plan. His promise is that
you will find Him when you search for Him. You're not supposed to seek Him only when you feel like it or are in dire
straits; He wants you to seek Him with all your heart in the
best of times and the worst of times.

You cannot search with all your heart without understanding that this is a daily process. Make up your mind to
search for Him every day. I thank God daily that in my worst
of times someone quoted Jeremiah 29:11–13 to me, and it lit
a fire in my soul. God literally spoke this word directly to
me through a person. I needed to hear that He was thinking
about me. I needed to know that He truly heard me when I
called His name.

I think this is the reason I am so passionate about giving
Jesus to everyone I meet. How can I dare just live a noncha-
lant life of pleasure when He took the time to direct me to
a passage of Scripture that changed my life? I realized there
are millions of people who are looking for that little ray of
hope just like I received that day. I want to give that hope
to them.

**SOMEBODY SOMEWHERE IS DEPENDING ON YOU TO DO
WHAT GOD HAS CALLED YOU TO DO.**
—*@RealTalkKim*

Sometimes we don't want to do the hard work. It is easier to rely on the pastor, our parents, or even friends to handle our decisions for us. However, God instructs each of us about our individual paths. When we ignore Him, we suffer, and the people around us suffer. By the mercies of God we are still breathing, but it is time to change!

Inconsistency, the mother of underachievement

Some people start out like balls of fire but end up like cold, wet snowballs. When they join your team, you recognize them as leaders in the making, but the longer you work with them, the more you see their mood fluctuations and lack of follow-through.

Something my dad has often said finally makes sense to me: "Oh consistency, thou art a jewel." Do you have friends who are different every time you see them? One day they are excited about the Paleo Diet. The next week they go vegan. You never know what to plan because their personalities and preferences change between visits.

Women, think about how your husband feels when he wonders each night whether you will be in your happy mood or that argumentative state that drives him into seclusion. Will he find you neatly dressed one day but looking like you just climbed out of bed the next? Do you wear the same old shirt three days in a row and wait a week to wash your hair? Why is it OK to present yourself to your husband that way but unacceptable to greet a stranger at the door in the same condition? If you had guests coming over, you know you would take a shower and look pretty for them.

Your husband would enjoy your time together so much more if you were consistent. He likes it when you fuss for him the way you do for outsiders. His compliments tell you that he needs you to look nice for him. Too many women with seductive spirits would be happy to dress up for your man. Let consistency be your friend!

Sir, the same goes for you. You cannot show your wife attention only on special occasions. What attracted her to you in the beginning? Whatever it was, keep doing it. You cannot underestimate the importance of consistency.

My parents are incredibly consistent. I have watched the way they live. Now in their fiftieth year of marriage, they are still smitten with each other. When I asked my mom why she loves my dad more now than she did fifty years ago, she shared several of his attributes. He always showers her with attention, even when he is busy building new congregations. When my brother and I lived at home, he always planned annual family vacations so we would know that he wasn't too busy for us. He always tells my mom how beautiful she is, even as she ages. And he still tells her fifty times a day how much he loves her. My dad is consistent.

I remember asking a former husband why he no longer complimented me, even though I was young and tried to look pretty for him. His answer was part of the baggage I had to release when I was cutting off soul ties. He said, "I don't need to compliment you now. I'm your husband."

His words devastated me because they said he no longer felt the need to love me and give me affection. Oh consistency, thou art a jewel!

You see, God created us to have fellowship, first with Him and then with each other. When communication fails, the relationship is over. When trust is lost, you cannot demand its return. Trust must be earned, and that takes consistency.

Even in church life there is a great need for members who are consistent in their love for God and ministry. Inconsistent people can be the biggest disappointment to ministry teams because although they have talents and gifts, they lack character. There is nothing worse than seeing the greatness in people stunted by their lack of character.

We dislike inconsistency, and God dislikes it too. He told the Laodicean church, "I know your works, that you are neither cold nor hot. I could wish you were cold or hot. So then, because you are lukewarm, and neither cold nor hot, I will vomit you out of My mouth" (Rev. 3:15–16). In other words, pick a temperature, and stick with it.

Why are people inconsistent even in church scenarios? Some are temperamental or unwilling to accept instruction. Others leave because someone criticized them. Have you been tempted to do that? Why is it easier to leave your church than to quit your job when someone hurts your feelings? How many times has your spouse offended you? Did you walk away? No. You went home and worked at the relationship. The same is true with your children. You know your children will hurt your feelings eventually, but you don't reject them, do you?

So why would you leave God's house because someone hurt your feelings? Your pastors are depending on you, yet you are determined to find another church because someone did you wrong. The enemy wants you to feel wounded. He's trying to steal your focus from the call of God on your life.

Promotion requires consistency. If you are not accomplishing your dreams or not being chosen for projects, take a look in the mirror. Is your follow-through weak? Was your last assignment incomplete? If so, you are probably inconsistent. It takes character to stick with the process. You have to start with a plan and then work it.

Consistency is also important when choosing your spouse. Looks fade. Every six-pack will be a one-pack someday. Don't waste your time on someone who is inconsistent about spending time with you. He promises to pick you up at a certain hour, but he is always late. She shows up the first time and stands you up twice after that. People like that are signaling that you are not special enough for them to keep their word.

Relationships are complex, and actions always cause

reactions. You cannot build strong relationships with people who do not value and model consistency.

Unbelief, the absence of faith

When you doubt yourself and God, you strangle your potential. Self-esteem, which is "confidence in one's own worth or abilities,"[5] cannot be found outside of yourself. Neither can your confidence in God. It comes from knowing and believing what God says about you.

PEOPLE WILL SEE YOUR WORTH WHEN YOU DO.
—*@RealTalkKim*

Do you have all the potential in the world—the education, personality, and leadership skills to become successful—yet seem to fail in your endeavors? You may be operating in unbelief. It is not enough for other people to believe in you. You must believe in yourself. A great example I often share involves one of my first cosmetics clients. On my first day at the job, she asked for a makeover. She had no idea that I was raised in a denomination where women wore no makeup.

When she sat at my station, I told her how beautiful she was and how she didn't need eyeliner or even eye shadow, just maybe a little lip gloss. Of course, I never mentioned that I had no idea how to apply eye makeup. I did the only thing I knew to do, which was build her up.

In the end she purchased a lip gloss.

I was shocked when she returned the next week. I knew I had not been the cosmetic expert she needed, yet there she was. She told me she was married twenty-eight years when her husband left her for another woman. Thirteen years had passed since her divorce, yet she still could not face being alone. She decided she was alone because she was not pretty or smart enough.

I knew none of this when I first met her and told her how

pretty her eyes and her high cheekbones were. She said that in thirteen years of counseling all she got were prescriptions for sleep and antidepression medications. Nothing worked until I shared some encouraging words. It lifted her up. She felt able to walk with her head high again. When she got home that day, she opened the blinds and let in the world again.

It doesn't matter what Negative Nelly says, as long as you believe in yourself and realize that God did not make you a nobody in your mother's womb. When you know that, you understand that you are one of a kind. No one else has your fingerprints. You cannot be duplicated. When you were created, God destroyed the mold.

You don't have to envy others or feel inferior to anyone. In my time of communion with God, I express my uniqueness by serving Him as only I can. I don't need people to build me up as I fellowship with my Creator. I talk to God, and then I talk to myself. When I declare that He is Lord over my life, I banish the fears and doubts that try to plague my mind. I renew my mind and recognize who I am in Christ. By the time I show up for that day's meetings with others, I know that I do not need them to define me. The Holy Spirit has already done that in my closet of prayer.

That is what frees me to succeed, in all things.

> Jesus said to him, "If you can believe, all things are possible to him who believes." Immediately the father of the child cried out and said with tears, "Lord, I believe; help my unbelief!"
>
> —MARK 9:23–24

All of us waver between faith and doubt at times. One moment you are standing on faith, believing for a miracle. The next moment something (however minor) throws you into a tailspin. I think the following verses are among the most important in counteracting Satan's ploys to stir doubt and unbelief.

> Though we walk in the flesh, we do not war according to the flesh. For the weapons of our warfare are not carnal but mighty in God for pulling down strongholds, casting down arguments and every high thing that exalts itself against the knowledge of God, bringing every thought into captivity to the obedience of Christ.
> —2 Corinthians 10:3–5

To understand how powerful this passage is, you must understand that when Paul wrote it, people were calling him weak and criticizing every facet of his life. He let them know that his weapons were not carnal. Therefore, he did not fight them in the physical. This is why the Bible says to pull down the imaginations of the mind and bring every thought into captivity to the obedience of Christ, who is the Word of God. You cannot fight the enemy on this level unless you know the Word of God.

MY AMMUNITION FOR EVERYTHING IN MY LIFE IS FAITH!
—@RealTalkKim

The enemy will do whatever he can to cripple your mind. When your mind is in a state of confusion, you cannot stand against his attacks. You are in a war, and you have spiritual weapons to counteract whatever the enemy uses against you. Your weapons are mighty through God. You have the promise of victory. But if you approach the situation you are facing with doubt, you choke off God's power.

Unbelief is about distrust and uncertainty. It makes you spiritually "bipolar," vacillating from one minute to the next. You try to evaluate issues by how things look. But things look different every day. How bad your circumstances are is not the issue. Where you see a mess, God sees a chance. Even if you have fallen back into unbelief, today is a new day. God has promised that if you consistently use His weapons, you can win. He has positioned you to change the game. What you deem a failure, God uses as a threshold into your next season.

That kind of hope will bind your enemy!

Will you allow your mess to move you forward? It is your decision to make!

> *Lord Jesus, create in me a clean heart and a pure mind. I invite You to be the Lord of my life, my situations, and my decisions. Help me to see myself as You see me.*

I DECLARE

I decree and declare that I am fearfully and wonderfully made. I will allow the Lord Jesus to turn my mess into a message. I will change my world.

CHAPTER 13

AGAINST ALL ODDS

T'S TIME TO move past your pain, accept His forgiveness, and change your future. When God breathes in your direction, closed doors fly open. You have a promised purpose, and only you can fulfill it.

My divorce, especially the second one, was supposed to disqualify me from ministry. When my family's denomination banished me to hell on a Slip 'N Slide, it did not realize I was already in the hell that I created for myself. We know hell as a place of perpetual torment and misery. My life was full of both. I realize that no "hell on earth" compares with the hell of eternity, but I can testify that my life was one miserable day followed by another. I had no peace and no joy. My self-esteem and identity were lost. *I* was lost.

It was the darkest season I had ever experienced, and I could not find my way out. Although I had experienced God many times in my life, I had never allowed Him to become a permanent resident in my heart. I used Him and abused Him, calling on Him when I needed Him but forsaking Him when times were good.

It took losing myself to find myself. I wanted to find a new me. Even I disliked the person I had become. I was so hardened by the cares of life and so reactive to every situation that I would not let anyone penetrate my heart. It was time to take care of *me*. I had been hurt so many times that

I believed I was the only one I could trust. Yet secretly I wasn't sure I could trust myself.

When I looked in the mirror, I could not believe who I had become. The person staring back at me knew that some people really loved her and wanted to be there for her. Yet she had locked herself so deep in a realm of bitterness and anger that she could not break free.

Finally I had to come to the end of myself, my feelings, and my beliefs. What did I really know about life? I had failed at two marriages, even after being raised to know that marriage was sacred. At the same time, I knew that God had deliberately blessed me. So I began thanking Him for His goodness to me, my boys, and my family.

It was still difficult to understand how anyone (especially God) could love the person I had become. Yet at just the right moments He brought into my life select people who believed in comebacks and makeovers. Through them God showed me that, against all odds, I could become a person full of peace, with a heart of flesh.

Gradually, He seasoned my heart of stone with love so I could learn to love others. I realize now that loving others means you must risk being hurt. No one is perfect. There *will* be times of disappointment and failure. Yet I discovered that I could walk in the forgiveness that allowed me to love others appropriately.

What I discovered through this process was a greater, more powerful, and more anointed me—the person God had ordained me to be before the foundation of the world. I believe that the enemy knew my purpose, which was written in God's book long before I was born. As the psalmist said, "Your eyes saw my substance, being yet unformed. And in Your book they all were written, the days fashioned for me, when as yet there were none of them" (Ps. 139:16).

I took those words personally!

You too have been called to a purpose by God. You are

uniquely formed and are unlike anyone else. The enemy of your future has been trying to keep you bound in order to steal your focus and prevent you from walking in your destiny. You don't have to let him.

Today I am so excited to know that I walked through a living hell and came out of it on fire. Even better, I know that if I can be free from all the bondages I allowed to overtake me, you can decide that your time for freedom has come.

WELCOME TO YOUR SETUP

As I travel from place to place to tell people how God's mercy gave me another chance, I feel like the most blessed person on this earth. When my family anxiously calls to make sure I am taking care of myself, I remind them that I spent thirty-six years living selfishly and God is now allowing me to love people back to life. I am never too tired, too frustrated, or too sick to pack my bags one more time and go tell others what my God has done.

IF YOU GO THROUGH HELL, COME OUT ON FIRE.
—*@RealTalkKim*

Man's plans are not God's plans. He has the best redemption plan in the universe. We all face challenges and experience tough times. Sometimes we feel stuck in a timeout with the odds unfairly stacked against us. The situations we face can seem like more than we can bear. Some of us (myself included) saw God as a mean, mean Father. We thought, "If He really loved me, I would not be experiencing all this hurt and rejection."

I was definitely there, wondering why my kids were losing their family and everything familiar to them. Those were hard times. Yet God used them to set me up for where He planned to take me in life and in ministry. When I finally grabbed hold of what He wanted to do in and through me, I no longer questioned or regretted my past or the many mistakes I had made. Instead, I began renewing my mind through prayer, praise, and worship. My purpose became my passion. My healing became a process that I absolutely refused to give up on. I decided there was no way I would go through that hell and not come out on fire for Him.

WE SERVE A GOOD, GOOD FATHER WHO WANTS TO HEAL EVERY ONE OF OUR HURTS.
—@RealTalkKim

These words are so real to me: "Beloved, I pray that you may prosper in all things and be in health, just as your soul prospers" (3 John 2). Because of my experiences with pain and rejection, I recognize both in the faces of people I encounter almost daily. I survived my past in order to lead many into a much greater future with God. So many who attend my meetings see them as a last resort. They have been abused by the world and even by the religious community. Their self-image is distorted, and their view of God is even less accurate.

The truth is that we serve a good, good Father who wants to heal every one of our hurts. The God I love and serve does not want any of His children to be broken or abused. He desires all to be healed and whole.

The story of the woman with the issue of blood parallels so many of our lives. She had been hemorrhaging for twelve long years. Can you imagine that? Some of us cannot bear even seven days of discomfort, and she was bleeding for twelve years! As you read her story, remember that your "issue" might not be physical. Maybe your emotions are out of control and causing you torment, or your family is falling apart. Whatever you are facing, this woman's experience is relevant to you.

Now a woman, having a flow of blood for twelve years, who had spent all her livelihood on physicians and could not be healed by any, came from behind and touched the border of His garment. And immediately her flow of blood stopped. And Jesus said, "Who touched Me?" When all denied it, Peter and those with him said, "Master, the multitudes throng and press You, and You say, 'Who touched Me?'"

But Jesus said, "Somebody touched Me, for I perceived power going out from Me." Now when the woman saw that she was not hidden, she came trembling; and falling down before Him, she declared to Him in the presence of all the people the reason she had touched Him and how she was healed immediately. And He said to her, "Daughter, be of good cheer; your faith has made you well. Go in peace."

—LUKE 8:43–48

This woman had done all she could and spent all she had. Yet she found no relief. Think about the physical effects of her affliction. She had lost so much blood that I think everyone could see how desperately sick she was. For her, the sickness went much deeper than its physical effects. In the Jewish law a bleeding woman was considered unclean and was prohibited from regular fellowship with others and even of going to worship God. According to the law, she should not have even ventured into the crowd.

Against all odds, she knew her only hope was for Jesus to touch her. There were many people pressing in to Jesus, however, and she was too frail to fight the crowd. Would you have been so determined to touch Jesus that you would crawl on your knees for one chance to grab the hem of His garment? This woman was! She did whatever was necessary to receive what no one had been able to give her for twelve long years.

It worked! When she touched Jesus' garment, He sensed the healing anointing leaving His body and knew that someone had touched Him by faith. With one touch the infirmity that imprisoned her for twelve years was over.

That can happen for you. God approved your healing more than two thousand years ago on Calvary. He also took thirty-nine stripes (or lashes) so you could be set free. By those stripes you are healed of all physical diseases and emotional conditions, as Isaiah prophesied long before the cross.

> He is despised and rejected by men, a Man of sorrows and acquainted with grief. And we hid, as it were, our faces from Him; He was despised, and we did not esteem Him. Surely, He has borne our griefs and carried our sorrows; yet we esteemed Him stricken, smitten by God, and afflicted. But He was wounded for our transgressions, He was bruised for our iniquities; the chastisement for our peace was upon Him, and by His stripes we are healed.
>
> —ISAIAH 53:3–5

Imagine—"He has borne our griefs and carried our sorrows"! Everything we could ever go through, Christ has experienced for us. There is no physical or emotional pain that He cannot heal. The man Jesus, who was despised and rejected by men, knew every sorrow and was no stranger to grief.

Again, this is about more than your physical healing. Jesus also breaks the chains of emotional and mental illness. Because my mom's family was cursed with mental illness, I have watched her declare her freedom from this disease throughout the years. My grandmother's mom passed away when she was very young, so her younger brothers and sisters had to be raised by the older siblings. Her story always made us weep as we tried to understand why my grandmother and her sisters battled emotional problems. Later my mom became a mother figure to her younger brother and sister as my grandmother battled a nervous condition that robbed years from her life.

My mom was determined that she would not allow that family curse to continue through our bloodline. Even through she experienced panic attacks, and even as the doctor prescribed medication for her, she refused to allow anything to rule her mind. She fed her mind with the Word of God and stayed in worship as she battled in that season. She read the many examples in the Word of God about miraculous healings and expected God to come through for her—and He did.

HEALING FOR THE HOPELESS

In my journey I have realized that hurt people hurt people and healed people heal people. After walking through the darkest season of my life, I began a journey that continues to this day. I will never "arrive" until I stand before God and He says, "Well done, good and faithful servant" (Matt. 25:21).

It's important for you to believe in God and believe that He will see you through your tough times. Your pain is real, but you can be free. It might take longer than a minute. I thought I would be pain-free within a year. However, it took six years for me to come to the end of myself, release all my pain and heartache, really forgive, and let it all go.

Today I can walk into a room and sense the pain and rejection that others are feeling. Their suffering is so real to me, but I offer them an even more real solution: Jesus Christ.

Daily I help walk men and women out of perilous conditions. God has ordained me to be a "hope dealer." When I can testify of His goodness in my life, it gives others hope in their hopeless situations.

You overcome the enemy by the blood of the Lamb and the word of your testimony—not by loving your life and your will but by pressing in to His. (See Revelation 12:11.) Your testimony is a weapon that rescues others from their battles of life and death. It will not be a tiptoe through the tulips, however. Just as Jesus has a plan for your life, Satan has a plot to kill, steal, and destroy you. You have to stand up for the abundant life you were promised. (See John 10:10.) I want that life and absolutely nothing less.

YOU CAN NEVER REALLY BE HEALED OR ACCOMPLISH GOD'S PURPOSE FOR YOU WITHOUT ALLOWING HIM TO BE YOUR LORD.
—@RealTalkKim

You want it too! When you get healed for real, you can see and enjoy the promise. That is when you learn to see others as Christ sees them. This earthly journey is not about being selfish and taking care of yourself. It is about serving others and giving of yourself so they can see the love of Christ through you.

Give Him permission to be the Lord of your life, spirit, soul, and body. I have learned and can testify that you can never really be healed or accomplish His purpose without allowing Him to be your Lord.

CRISES CONQUERED

While living with my parents as a teenager, I was so protected that I lost sight of reality and believed I could succeed even on an island alone. I created that island by shutting out everyone on whom I had depended. As long as I had money in my pocket, I thought I would make it. God, however, knew how to get my attention.

My one constant in life was knowing that my parents were praying for me. During the failure of my second marriage, I realized that I could not hide under the covers forever, waiting for my crisis to be over. At the time, everything was in crisis. Having long since moved out from under my parents' covering, I now wanted that security one more time. At thirty-six years of age, I hadn't been under my parents' covering for eighteen years, so we all were walking down a strange new path.

Although I was not the daughter my parents expected me to be, I knew they would be there when I needed them. At the same time, I began to understand that I could not recover on my own. I had failed miserably at being my own hero. It was time for me to get up, start fresh, and walk away from everything that had been holding me back. The odds seemed to be against me, but I knew I would make it.

I don't know what your issues look like. Maybe your husband of twenty-five years walked out on you or you lost a baby or made poor financial decisions. There is no situation so great that God's love cannot cover it. Paul said, "In all these things we are more than conquerors through Him who loved us" (Rom. 8:37).

That is a powerful declaration of freedom and victory. It says you never again have to be bound by your mistakes. The hurt that was done to you by your father, mother, sister, or brother is not the final word either. Friends who betrayed you are no longer part of your future. They were mere contributors to the amazing destiny God has planned. You can be freed from the crises of both your past and present. Believe it, and declare right now, *"No more*! My crises are over and I am free."

You may be facing similar odds to those I have experienced. You may have set those odds against yourself, as I did.

When I left home at eighteen years of age, I was certain that I could take my world by force. I thought I did not need my family or church. I thought I could propel myself into greatness. Even in high school I had proved to myself that I could make it. I was hired part time at Macy's and decided to be its best employee ever. I worked my way into a full-time position while attending school. My dream had always been to own a BMW. I purchased a used BMW and thought it was the deal of the century. I did not need anybody's help or guidance (or so I thought). I was my own best friend, counselor, and financial planner. It was all about me.

After high school I married my boyfriend of two years, and we immediately moved to another country. The girl who was convinced she could accomplish anything found herself in a foreign land dependent on everyone for everything. I could not speak the language or even drive my car (which my husband and I had purposely driven there, hoping I could pass that country's driver's test).

After realizing I could not even read the language well enough to take a test, I knew there was no way I could be the independent, self-sufficient woman I thought I could be. Reality hit me hard. This was accompanied by depression. How in the world did I ever think I could be two thousand miles away from my family in a place where I knew only my husband and his parents? I had left behind all my friends and my freedom.

I had not bothered to think this move through until it was too late. I kept telling myself that the decision had been made and I would need to make the most of it. But loneliness began to plague me, and I could think of only one thing: I needed my family.

My parents' phone rang many times at two in the morning. They awakened to hear my desperate sobs; fears of the unknown; and fears of people, places, and things. My dad would talk me through my anxiety and then sweetly remind me that they were in Atlanta, which was eight hours away by air. There was nothing they could do to help me in the middle of the night.

I felt the odds stacking higher against me. Why in the world did I think I could leave home and make a life outside of the security my parents had given me? As they built churches, pastored congregations, and provided a great home for my brother and me, they made life look so easy. Then the realization hit me: although I believed I had accomplished everything on my own, none of it could have happened without the covering of godly parents and their prayers.

Because of my immaturity it was hard to see how God would use my pain and fear to guide me toward His purpose despite my foolish decisions. Nevertheless, I had a spirit of endurance and believed that though I was down for the moment, I would be up and moving forward the next day. I am thankful for that.

Perseverance is the key to breakthrough. Scripture says, "Do not cast away your confidence, which has great reward. For you have need of endurance, so that after you have done the will of God, you may receive the promise" (Heb. 10:35–36). We tend to stop short of what God has promised us, giving up right before we reach it. We allow fear to paralyze us and stunt our progress. We lose sight of our purpose and dreams. What we need is the mind-set to persevere until we see the promises of God manifested in our lives.

Because you are reading this book, I know you are set on "Go" to see a tomorrow unlike anything you have experienced so far. The key is perseverance, the simple decision to get up one more time than you fall down. You have to forgive those who have maliciously wounded you and love those who are unlovable. You hurt only yourself when you allow other people's judgments to rule you. I can remember telling God that I wanted to defend myself against the malicious gossip of others. He said, "Live as though the stories they are telling are untrue. Let Me vindicate you."

PERSEVERANCE IS THE SIMPLE DECISION TO GET UP ONE MORE TIME THAN YOU FALL DOWN.
—@RealTalkKim

This directive changed my life. I got so busy living a new life that I refused to allow anyone to pull me back into my old one.

ALL THINGS WORK TOGETHER

Four months after getting married, leaving my parents' house, and moving to another country, God gave us a way out. My husband was offered a job back in the United States, and we were able to begin again in Columbus, Ohio. If you had told me then that God was doing a miraculous work in me, I would have laughed in your face. How could this simple move set me up for a breakthrough twenty-five years later? Yet in the past year I watched God reopen a door that I had closed back then.

"All the promises of God in Him are Yes, and in Him Amen, to the glory of God through us" (2 Cor. 1:20). We have to make up our minds and hearts that no matter how difficult the journey, we will not give in or give up.

There is a story in Joshua 6 that captures the essence of that kind of passion. In the story we learn that God promised the land beyond the Jordan River to His people, but they were not yet in possession of it. Remember that these were the people who continually grumbled and complained when things did not seem to go their way. As a result of their refusal to persevere, a whole generation died before reaching the Promised Land.

The same thing can happen to us when we forget another amazing promise: "Blessed be the God and Father of our

Lord Jesus Christ, who has blessed us with *every spiritual blessing* in the heavenly places in Christ" (Eph. 1:3). That tells me that everything found in Christ should be operating in our lives, all the time. His strength, peace, joy, love, favor, and power are available. However, we have to fight the fight of faith to possess and live in the promise. Always, the war is in the mind, or soul.

In Joshua 6 we see that God allowed the children of Israel to go through many challenges, yet He gave them a way out of each one.

> Now Jericho was securely shut up because of the children of Israel; none went out, and none came in. And the LORD said to Joshua: "See! I have given Jericho into your hand, its king, and the mighty men of valor. You shall march around the city, all you men of war; you shall go all around the city once. This you shall do six days. And seven priests shall bear seven trumpets of rams' horns before the ark. But the seventh day you shall march around the city seven times, and the priests shall blow the trumpets. It shall come to pass, when they make a long blast with the ram's horn, and when you hear the sound of the trumpet, that all the people shall shout with a great shout; then the wall of the city will fall down flat. And the people shall go up every man straight before him."
>
> —JOSHUA 6:1–5

God's promise and instructions were *amazing*. We are about to see how the Jericho battle turned out and why my Ohio story included defeat and victory.

A MATTER OF PERSPECTIVE

People stop short because their perspective gets blocked. The Israelites were about to possess the very land God first promised to Abraham, Isaac, Jacob, and Moses, but before they possessed it, they had to march. I remember in Sunday school singing the little chorus about the walls that came tumbling down in Jericho. I honestly think we oversimplified the battle with that song.

Jericho was the first city to be conquered. In my opinion, the first one is always the hardest. Getting started is half the battle. Joshua spent forty years in the wilderness before having the opportunity to fight for Jericho, and I believe the battle was not as simple as we make it sound. We always assume that other people's victories were easy for them. I can tell you that no one knows the cost of my journey to be where I am today, and no one knows yours.

After my first husband and I moved to Columbus, we were invited to a church called World Harvest, pastored by Rod Parsley. We had no idea where that decision would lead. My husband's job kept him out of town each week. Meanwhile I had no friends in Columbus, so I got involved in the music program. God instilled in me a passion for music. He also gave me the opportunity to sing on the front line of this powerful team. I even traveled with Pastor Parsley for his citywide crusades.

It was an amazing year, during which I sensed a stirring inside of me. Yet I watched my marriage unravel day by day. We sought counsel, trying to keep our relationship together. However, it eventually failed.

Because I was on the worship team, church leaders were there to help me walk through that loss. However, Satan immediately set me up for failure. A young man began to pursue me feverishly. At the time, I felt as if I needed that kind of attention. My pastor warned me that if I kept heading in that direction, I would be "jumping out of the frying pan and into the fire." I wondered how he could even imagine that I would make such a stupid decision. So once again, I decided it was time for a change. I packed my bags and moved on, with the next young man in tow.

The pastor was right. That decision set up years of disobedience and altered the dynamics of my family. My parents were distraught. They let me know they loved me but opposed my decisions. It didn't matter to me. My perspective was clouded, and I went from one bad move to another. My perspective was so skewed that I was convinced I was right. The door God opened for me to sing on the worship team and travel as a team member with the pastor had now closed. I didn't even glance back at what I was missing.

No wonder the story of Jericho and the Israelites is so special to me today! The lesson that stands out most is seeing how well the Israelites listened to their leader. I had never listened to anyone who told me how to possess God's purposes.

IF YOU ARE FOCUSED ON THE WALLS, SETBACKS, AND PROBLEMS AROUND YOU, YOU WILL NEVER POSSESS THE PROMISES OF GOD.
—*@RealTalkKim*

Jericho was a small city. Walking around it only took about an hour. Israel thought the problem was the size of the wall. We think the same way. We focus on the obstacles between us and God's promises. But God in us is greater than the obstacles and enemies we face. (See 1 John 4:4.) This is why worship is so important. It helps us get God's perspective so we can see over the walls around us and beyond the opposition.

If you are focused on the walls, setbacks, and problems around you, you will never possess the promises of God. But if you worship Him, your perspective will change. You will believe that nothing is too hard for God.

David, the consummate worshipper, learned this lesson early and wrote about it, saying:

> I will bless the LORD at all times; His praise shall continually be in my mouth. My soul shall make its boast in the LORD; the humble shall hear of it and be glad. Oh, magnify the LORD with me, and let us exalt His name together.
>
> —PSALM 34:1–3

Come into the Lord's presence and allow Him to fill you up. You will find that your intimidator was intimidated by you the whole time.

Let's read the first two verses of Joshua 6 again:

> Now Jericho was securely shut up because of the children of Israel; none went out, and none came in. And the LORD said to Joshua: "See! I have given Jericho into your hand, its king, and the mighty men of valor."
>
> —JOSHUA 6:1–2

Jericho was locked up tight, but God was already speaking victory to Joshua. Only God can speak in the past tense about a battle yet to be fought. He did it in Jericho, and He's done it in my life. He saw the eighteen years ahead of me and knew how they would end. He was not stressed about the things that were stressing me. From outside of time He told me how to get in line with His plan.

Still, I thought I had everything figured out. I would marry again and live a fairy-tale love affair. That was my lifelong dream, but it was not to be. Even when things looked good on the outside, I knew I would have to face the truth one day.

Have you been there? Is your life not matching up with what God promised? Are you sensing a wake-up call ahead? Stories about real people who faced real challenges and came through it all will help you. The Jericho story is one of them. Because it was so huge, the wall was all the people of Israel could see—not the enemy behind the wall, just the wall. As intimidating as the wall was, Joshua had to trust God totally.

Have you sensed God speaking victory, but still you see defeat ahead? I'm asking because this happens and will continue to happen. God wants us to trust Him all the way to victory. What God shows us may look completely different from what's actually in front of us. We need people who can help us see over our walls, and we need to understand what we are seeing. The wall is not a wall at all. It is a call to a higher plane of living.

Joshua understood that. When he received God's instructions, he went to the people.

> Then Joshua the son of Nun called the priests and said to them, "Take up the ark of the covenant, and let seven priests bear seven trumpets of rams' horns before the ark of the LORD." And he said to the people, "Proceed, and march around the city, and let him who is armed advance before the ark of the LORD."...Now Joshua had commanded the people, saying, "You shall not shout or make any noise with your voice, nor shall a word proceed out of your mouth, until the day I say to you, 'Shout!' Then you shall shout." So he had the ark of the LORD circle the city, going around it once. Then they came into the camp and lodged in the camp....And the

second day they marched around the city once and returned to the camp. So they did six days.

—JOSHUA 6:6–7, 10–11, 14

Remember that the fighting men went first. They thought they were going to war, but God instructed them to take a walk. Six days in, there seemed to be no progress. If I were God, I would have given the Israelites a sign on the first day. They had been wandering in the wilderness for more than forty years and had not seen evidence of the promise coming to pass.

YOU'VE BEEN TELLING GOD HOW BIG YOUR MOUNTAIN IS—
IT'S TIME TO TELL YOUR MOUNTAIN HOW BIG YOUR GOD IS!
—*@RealTalkKim*

And now they needed to take a walk?

One more day might not sound like a big deal, but to the Israelites it must have been torture. Plus, Joshua told them not to make a sound. Their mouths had always gotten them in trouble with God and Moses. Joshua probably feared that their thoughts and words would keep them out of the Promised Land.

I am sure my need for signs kept me out of step with God. I was the type who needed proof of my progress. Yet that isn't how God operates. The Israelites obeyed for six days without seeing any change. Joshua did not say how long they would have to march. He just told them to march.

So they marched, and what happened changed everything.

It came to pass on the seventh day that they rose early, about the dawning of the day, and marched around the city seven times in the same manner. On that day only they marched around the city seven times. And the seventh time it happened,

> when the priests blew the trumpets, that Joshua said to the people: "Shout, for the LORD has given you the city!"...So the people shouted when the priests blew the trumpets. And it happened when the people heard the sound of the trumpet, and the people shouted with a great shout, that the wall fell down flat. Then the people went up into the city, every man straight before him, and they took the city.
>
> —JOSHUA 6:15–16, 20

God doesn't tell you in advance when your dreams will be fulfilled. You don't know the date of your future husband's appearance or the day your ship will come in. God wants to know that you will trust Him every step of the way, even when there is no sign.

Do you believe God is working even when your efforts seem fruitless? Will you wait patiently and keep praying, serving, and giving? Will you march simply because God told you to march? Remember that consistency requires faith. If eating right or working out produced immediate results, everyone would do it. If eating one carrot could firm up your abs, we would all be eating carrots instead of ordering pizza.

That is not how it works, however. Results are not instantaneous. Bodybuilders spend years creating chiseled physiques. We think we would give anything to be built like them—anything except spending hours in the gym each day and running thirty or more miles each week.

When the Israelites walked around Jericho, God was preparing them to fight the giants in the land. They had to play a part in taking what God had promised. It's no different for us. As we serve in God's house, He prepares us to handle the greater things He is calling us to do.

Looking back to my years of failure, I can see that God was preparing me for bigger things. He was never hidden from my life. No matter how bad things looked, He was always there. When I moved back into my parents' home and took five more years to surrender to Him, He waited. When I finally allowed Him to change me, He said, "Yes."

One of my favorite testimonies is quite recent. I was invited to speak at World Harvest during their Dominion Camp Meeting! Years earlier, when I was on the church's worship team, the Dominion conference was the premier event of the season. We were awed by every speaker and could hardly wait for each service. When I received the call to speak at the conference, the Lord revealed how I had (figuratively) marched around that wall for twenty-five years since leaving World Harvest in rebellion. I could never have dreamed that I would stand on that platform again, but God knew. He prepared me. All I had to do was persevere.

EVERYTHING YOU'VE BEEN THROUGH
IS WORKING FOR YOUR GOOD.
—@RealTalkKim

God has been setting you up. Against all odds, He is leading you to your promised land. Only He can redeem your failures. Only He can give you a platform that you could never imagine or arrange. But waiting is involved. He is more concerned about your character than your comfort, more concerned about what He is doing on your inside than what you are doing on the outside.

So don't quit. You might be doing the sixth lap around your wall. It might be painful. This might be your most difficult year ever. Maybe your friends have no clue about your turmoil. But God knows, and He wants you to keep moving. Breakthrough is on the horizon. You will make it, against all odds.

Lord Jesus, I humbly come to You confessing my failures and asking You for complete restoration. Allow me to become the vessel You called me to be. You are the Lord of my life, and my strength.

I DECLARE

I decree and declare that I will see life change. I will allow the Lord Jesus to rule and reign over every decision I make for my life. I am called, chosen, and faithful.

CHAPTER 14

GO FOR IT!

AT SOME POINT in your life the people who love you will say, "Go for it!" Yet your greatest cheerleaders can also become your toughest critics. When you move one step forward and two steps back, even you will question your decisions, your reasoning, and God's will for your life. You'll be like the turtle I mentioned in chapter 1 that trudges through peanut butter and makes slow progress.

When your efforts seem to add up to nothing and freedom seems to move further away, you need to understand why your enemy is fighting you. It's not because you are weak but because you are strong. Realizing that will help you stand firm and make more life-changing decisions. Achieving success still won't be easy, and you'll be tempted to give up at times. However, earning a degree, launching a business, forming a small group, or starting over after a divorce or death in the family are worthwhile goals. All you need is faith in God and yourself to accomplish them.

When you choose to change, you will go through a process. God is shifting you so you can continue to grow, but that won't always be comfortable. Using the five letters in the word *shift*, I want to look at what is happening during this time of transition.

- **Synchrony**—This refers to chronological events that are parallel. In the midst of your chaos and confusion, God is establishing order in your life. Where there is disaster and disappointment, God is providing prosperity. Both are happening at the same time. Even in my lack God was working to bring me into the most prosperous season of my life. We must remember that "all things work together for good to those who love God, to those who are the called according to His purpose" (Rom. 8:28).

THE ENEMY ISN'T FIGHTING YOU BECAUSE YOU ARE WEAK
BUT BECAUSE YOU ARE STRONG!
—@RealTalkKim

- **Humility**—Most of us will say that we are humble, but I think few people truly understand humility until God begins to shift us. I know now that I had no idea what humility truly was before God began to transform me. I was always about designers and labels and fine cars until I hit my bottom. The simplest way to define *humility* is as the ability to go low. Humility says this shift isn't about me, but it's definitely for me. During a shift God brings us to the end of ourselves, our dreams, and our passions so we will look to Him for His purpose for our lives. When we come to this place of humility, we will be ready for Him to complete His work in us.

- **Isolation**—When a shift happens, you will find yourself isolated. Often this is because God is preparing you for the next phase.

Before Moses was to lead the Israelites out of captivity, he was isolated in the wilderness. Joseph was to help supply food to his family during a terrible famine, but he was isolated from them for many years. This period of isolation is necessary for the shift in your life to be made complete. In this time of isolation you spend an exponential amount of time alone with God. This is when you begin to recognize His voice and become acquainted with the One we call Lord.

- **Fumigation**—We discussed this necessary action in chapter 10, but I want to say here that the people you release from your life are not necessarily bad people. The people who left my world during my journey were not bad people; they just were not part of the next season in my life. Rarely does every character in a movie appear in every scene. In fact, some appear only at the beginning. Trust God when He moves people out of your life, and be pliable as He works His will in you. God knows what is best for you.

- **Transformation**—This is the evidence that a shift has taken place in and around us. Our minds—the way in which we think—will be completely changed. The old things will have passed away, and we will become new. And because our identity has changed, our environment will also change.

As your shift happens, don't stop moving forward. Even if you feel as though you have "the worst" past, you can create a great future. Ecclesiastes 9:11 says the race is not given to the swift, nor is the battle necessarily won by the strong. Yet enduring to the end is a victory of its own. So be prepared to endure. Your endurance might not win you the race, but it will ensure that you finish it.

STOP TRYING TO RECYCLE WHAT GOD IS TRYING TO REPLACE.
—@RealTalkKim

When God puts in your heart the desire to do something, you cannot let anyone or anything stop you. Success requires tremendous effort, but through His power you can succeed. Hurts and disappointments might come, but nothing can keep you from completing your task, unless you let it.

I can testify to that! Change and success have demanded much effort, but when I realized that I could make it with God's help, nothing could draw me away.

It is no different for you. You will be tempted to worry, but worry is a waste of your time. Don't try to figure out your situations. That journey will only take you from somewhere to absolutely nowhere. Just realize that you don't know everything God knows about what's going on. He will see you through.

When you decide to make changes, your first question might be, "What will people think?" My advice is to focus less on what people think about you and more on what God knows about you. He is the One who called you, and no one knows all that He does.

And what about the cost of going for it? Is it too much to handle? Will it do you in? Not if you are doing what God asks. Do you remember the woman with the alabaster flask? The perfume she poured out on Jesus was worth a year's salary. (See Mark 14:3–9.) Yet she poured it freely to anoint Him for His death and burial. She showed us what sacrifice looks like by offering what was most precious to her. That was her legacy. Although people pointed at her and whispered about her, she fulfilled her purpose. One decision set up a life change that no amount of education or financial success could have given her.

When you choose to go for it, remember that things are seldom as they seem. If you worry your way through life, you will become accustomed to a negative outlook. The truth is that you cannot control everything, and situations are rarely as bad as you think they are. The woman with the alabaster flask could have been paralyzed by other people's judgments. Instead, she focused on the eternal, despite her insecurities and fears.

I encourage you to have a similar mind-set. Let your faith direct your life.

ARE YOU READY?

Two thousand years ago on the Day of Pentecost, 120 people changed the world. If 120 everyday people could do that in Jerusalem, God can use you to shake up your world, your family, your church, and your workplace. You can say, "I'm waiting on God to move," but He is waiting on you to move. All your life He has been waiting for you to focus on Him and walk out His plan.

Sometimes God makes you wait. If He gave you what you prayed for when you first asked, you would have messed up. He did you a favor when He slowed you down. You can't always handle the scope of God's blessing just because you have asked for it. God gives your character a chance to catch up with the greatness of His plan.

His plan *is* great, and He has a major purpose for every human life. Are you ready for it? Is your character right? If a door opened today for the major platform He showed you, would you stay humble or walk in pride? When you gain influence, will you point people to Jesus or to yourself? If

God gives you a spouse, will you be selfless and ready to forgive a million times a day? Will you love your spouse when your flesh wants to fight? Or will you insist on having your way?

STOP ASKING EVERYONE'S OPINION. ASK GOD WHAT HE THINKS!
—@RealTalkKim

After being anointed as Israel's king, David modeled the utmost submission. Instead of going directly to the throne, he returned to the fields with his father's sheep. God knew David wasn't ready to replace King Saul. He had to undergo a process, which prepared him for his purpose in God.

There is a process for you too. People might see your waiting time as a season of failure, but God ordained it for your future. Success might elude you for a day or even years, but when the time comes, the circumstances will fit together perfectly. People on the outside will say your success was sudden, but you will know that God hid you and molded you as His vessel.

Many people think I fell into success as a pulpit minister. To think it "just happened" is an understatement of the facts. A lot occurred, and after losing my husband, home, and business, I had no clue how to approach life or Jesus. All I knew to do was move in with my folks and put my furniture in storage units I could not afford. I went to my room each night feeling as if I had disappointed everyone who meant anything to me. I wondered how I would ever recover all that was lost.

My worrying was all about me. It had nothing to do with faith or a godly perspective. From my thinking to my actions, everything needed to change. And that was more challenging than I could have imagined.

FAITHFUL, NO MATTER WHAT

For the record, I know that millions of people go through divorce and loss each year. However, when it happens in your family, the devastation is overwhelming. I began seeking God faithfully. It was the only way I could find myself. Yet faithfulness did not come easily. As a woman raised in a preacher's home, I watched my parents trust God in every facet of life. Yet I somehow lost my connection to the family legacy. I suppose the truth is that I rejected it and the call to ministry for many years.

After almost two decades of wandering, I began my restoration journey. It was not an overnight thing. Faithfulness takes time to develop. The late Edwin Louis Cole wrote, "Faithfulness is a mark of maturity. Constancy, loyalty and strength are its evidence. God requires men to be faithful."[1]

That is how my parents raised me: to be faithful. I was on the church pew during every service and in the prayer room with my mother an hour before service started. Mom insisted that I accompany her. She could not make me pray, but she wanted me to be in the life-changing atmosphere of prayer.

One of my most vivid childhood memories is of hearing my mom travail before God in that prayer room. Sadly I misunderstood what was going on. I imagined that God was harsh and difficult to reach. Why else would my mom have to cry and beg for His help?

I would not understand until I returned home and heard my parents praying for my boys and me. Even then it took a while to sink in. I thought, "How can they stand in faith when they see that I have lost everything? Don't they know that I am messed up from the floor up? Doesn't that embarrass them in front of their church family and other Christian friends?" I thought parents liked to brag about their kids and give God the glory for their accomplishments. Yet when the subject of Kimberly came up, my parents had nothing to brag about.

Still, I remember listening one day as they spoke of me, not with embarrassment but with the love and pride that only parents have. They *always* talked about me that way. I wondered, "How can they do that when they're covering all my bills and even my boys' schooling?"

As I meditated in my room one night, I received understanding of how my parents managed to stand so strong and in such peace when their world was shaken. It was because they had been faithful to stay in God's presence during their best and most prosperous seasons. Then when a dark season came, they knew God would come through. Even today my parents (who have had some torturous battles in their walk with God) stand firm, believing that He will be with them always.

My parents were faithful in every way, including in the way they nurtured my brother and me. I sang from childhood into adulthood. I had gifts and talents that everyone recognized as exceptional. I was the soloist who captivated the congregation. My mom made sure I had voice lessons and whatever was needed to ensure that my gifts made room for me, as Proverbs 18:16 says. At the time, I did not realize that I needed character, not just ability. Ability is built on talent and practice, but character is built on faithfulness.

KNOWING GOD AND SUBMITTING

When you enter into relationship with God and uncover the riches of knowing Him, you will do anything to know Him better. So you start reading His Word, praying, and serving. That is when you discover what the apostle Paul meant when he said that "all the treasures of wisdom and knowledge" are hidden in Christ (Col. 2:3).

The better we know God, the more we reflect Him. When

my life fell apart, I realized that I desperately needed intimacy with Jesus Christ. My lack of intimacy with Him was affecting me and everyone around me. Faith, hope, and love were either going to show up in my actions and relationships, or they weren't. The latter prospect was not a good one. The wrong choice would hurt all of us for a very long time.

THE BETTER WE KNOW GOD, THE MORE WE REFLECT HIM.
—@RealTalkKim

You can learn about God while listening to someone preach, but you become personally acquainted with His love when you get alone with Him. I began a journey of aloneness. I remembered my mom's example in the prayer room at church. She did not care who heard her pleadings. She simply yielded everything to Jesus and trusted Him to set things right. Now I was ready to do the same—to surrender everything to find the Savior who gave His life for me.

God is no respecter of persons and shows no partiality. (See Acts 10:34, kjv, and Romans 2:11.) To receive something I never had, I had to make some changes, beginning with my mind. It was a formative season. Later my parents admitted how desperately they wanted to intervene as I cried out to God. They longed to nurture me as they always had. However, God said, "Leave her alone."

I was getting to know my God, and He was preparing me for His use. The only thing I needed to do was submit. Only He could make it happen. The One who called me was and is faithful. (See 1 Thessalonians 5:24.)

It is all about submission. You are uniquely called, and you will respond uniquely. Almost thirty years ago, John Mason explained the importance of being ourselves:

> In this day of peer pressure, trends, and fads, we
> need to realize and accept that each person has

been custom-made by God the Creator. Each of us
has a unique and personal call upon our lives. We
are to be our own selves and not copy other people.[2]

We are fearfully and wonderfully made by God. (See
Psalm 139:14.) We owe it to ourselves and to Him to become
our best selves, using our talents for something beautiful and
worthy. Submitting to Him this way takes staying power.
That staying power is faithfulness, and it is supported by
vision and determination.

Everyone has moments of wavering or indecision. But
know this: when you are undecided, you can be easily
swayed. When you are determined and decide, for example,
that your crisis is temporary and your family will make it,
Satan cannot not steal your joy or rob your blessings. When
you remain committed to your decision, no force in hell can
take you down.

I remember realizing that I absolutely had to take a stand.
Despite my upbringing I never really had a relationship with
Jesus Christ. I knew very little about the Bible and very little
about God. So I purchased a children's picture Bible (seri-
ously!) and learned the stories most Christians already knew.
I wanted to know everything about God and why He chose
me to change my world. That meant starting with His Word,
which is Jesus Christ Himself. (See John 1:1–5.)

Until I knew His Word, I could not know God. My
journey to know Jesus as my Lord and Savior had begun. I
would soon meet the One who "[upholds] all things by the
word of His power" (Heb. 1:3).

SMALL BEGINNINGS

These are different times than we have ever known, and we
face decisions we have never faced before. Our daily cry

must be, "Thy will be done in earth, as it is in heaven" (Matt. 6:10, kjv).

As I searched for my place in God's kingdom, I wondered, "Why did God make me? And how can I love, serve, and obey Him today?" My only platform at the time was the cosmetics counter at Bloomingdale's. But there was no rushing God. He would proceed in whatever timing was suitable while He had me in the darkroom of my life. He was developing me, and I had to trust Him.

SMALL BEGINNINGS CAN LEAD TO UNIMAGINED PLACES WHEN WE SUBMIT OUR WILL TO GOD.
—*@RealTalkKim*

Still, I wondered how God would give a broken vessel like me a reason to live. I wanted Him to flow through me. My shame was still very real, but I had to release it. The longer it ruled me, the more unholy it would become. Knowing that God loved me despite even my future mistakes freed me to focus on my new beginning. I could now forgive myself for the messes I had allowed and make righteous decisions for my future. I was being freed to serve Him.

Small beginnings can lead to unimagined places when we submit our will to God. That is how "ordinary" people do the most amazing things.

World Vision President Richard Stearns wrote in *The Hole in Our Gospel*:

> Mother Teresa is widely attributed as having said, "I am a little pencil in the hand of a writing God who is sending a love letter to the world." She had it right. We are not authors, any of us. We are just the "pencils." Once we understand that, we might actually become useful to God.[3]

Being that pencil is such a privilege! It requires our learning the story that the author and finisher of our faith wants to write. During my one-hour commute to and from the cosmetics counter each day, I listened to the great preachers who were setting our nation on fire. I did not realize that those hours were a part of the education God would use to catapult me into international ministry.

Here I was, someone who had always been quick to express my opinion, choosing to be quiet and listen. Listening helped me learn more about God's purpose for my pain. Yet I was so eager to do His will and pass His test—maybe a little too eager! When I finally told my dad (who was also my pastor) that I was ready to speak publicly, he smiled and said, "Not yet, baby girl."

The delay frustrated me because I believed I was ready. But my dad was right, and God knew best. Listening to preachers was only part of the "curriculum" I had to complete. To become a voice for broken vessels worldwide, I had to learn how to listen to other people's pain.

Listening is critical! As John Mason wrote, "Hearing tells you that the music is playing; listening tells you what the song is saying."[4] Isn't that brilliant? Here's another gem: "One of the least developed skills among us human beings is that of listening. There are really two different kinds of listening. There is the natural listening in interaction with other people, and there is spiritual listening to the voice of God."[5]

Until my life crashed, I did not know God's voice. Afterward I became so hungry for Him that I could barely wait to meet with Him each day. Those one-on-ones were first and foremost for the sake of loving Him. But meeting with Him also changed me and took me to new places as a person. I began to understand my troubled times and transitions. Something Edwin Cole said has changed the way I see them.

> One of the greatest passages in the Bible, repeated
> often by various writers, is "it came to pass." It's a
> statement of transition, meaning that something
> occurred at a particular time. Its meaning is doubly
> true when we realize things come to "pass," not to
> "stay." *Nothing that has come to you in life came to stay;*
> *it all came to pass.*[6]

That is life changing! Situations and conditions come, *and*
they go. Change is always possible. Cole talks about how we
let temporary issues stress us out but discover glory in what
is permanent and eternal. He reminds us that God is more
interested in where He is taking us than what we are leaving
behind.[7] He always sees the end from the beginning. (See
Isaiah 46:9–10.)

What God desires in all of this is a personal relationship
with us. That is our primary purpose—fellowship with the
Creator. We discover His pattern for our lives when we are
all alone with Him. In those times we develop a sensitivity
to His voice that is unlike anything found anywhere, even in
Bible school training.

God's Word is your blueprint for success. Don't be tossed to
and fro by every whim, personality, feeling, or fleeting thought
that comes along. Steady yourself in the Word of God.

When I was alone with God in my bedroom at my parents' house, I did not expect what eventually came to pass.
Now, because God has provided an international platform, I
am determined to share what He gives me with others. How
long will my season last? I don't know, but I know this is
my season.

You also have a season. When you feel as if you are alone
and your faith is nowhere, God is still faithful. Let Him
fine-tune you. He loves you and will never fail you. He does
not lead you toward negative pathways or dead ends. He is

not looking to punish or humiliate you. He will, however, allow certain pressures to mature and prepare you for greater service.

God did that for me, as undeserving as I was. Therefore, I am willing to expose the old skeletons in my closet for your sake. I pray daily for Jesus to use my brokenness and make me a strong willow that bends with the wind. I can relate to David and marvel at his dynamic relationship with God. I am encouraged by how beautifully God shaped his life. Israel's future king knew he wasn't alone. He rejoiced to draw close to God and receive His wisdom. He knew he could not run from God or His justice, and he knew he could count on His power. (See Psalms 18:1–2; 23:3–4; and 139:7–10.)

God honored David's faith and spoke highly of Him:

> And when He had removed him [Saul], He raised up for them David as king, to whom also He gave testimony and said, "I have found David the son of Jesse, a man after My own heart, who will do all My will."
>
> —Acts 13:22, kjv

God has a way of drawing you away from distractions and into His will. If you allow Him to strip away your baggage, He will focus you on your calling, which is holy and personal. You must say yes, however. No one can determine your current choices or end results. Only you can accept your calling and separate yourself from the weights of life. The choice is a powerful one, and you can make it.

It is a matter of choosing to flow with what God has on His agenda. That means being flexible and putting His preferences over yours. You can pass the tests that come your way because you can keep your "textbook" open! He gave you His Word so you could prepare ahead of time and draw on His wisdom at a moment's notice.

There will be bumps and bruises along the way. Adversity comes to everyone. You don't have to go looking for it. It will find you. The important thing is how you respond to it. Know that God is with you in *everything*, shaping and forming you into the person you are becoming, the one He destined from the beginning.

You cannot know everything that is ahead, but you can be sure that change is coming. Don't set your plans in stone. Respond nimbly to your heavenly Father. In the long run what you have planned can never be as good as His plan. So follow Him. Some things will take longer to change than you first hoped. Other things will change in the twinkling of an eye. Either way, God's timing will prevail.

Success may elude you for a season, a day, or a year, but when the right time comes, all the circumstances will come into alignment. So keep on keeping on. When hurts and disappointments come, set your jaw and say, "Nothing can keep me from walking out God's plan for my life. *Nothing*."

YOUR CURRENT SITUATION IS NOT YOUR FINAL DESTINATION!
—@RealTalkKim

Remember that every success story is a blend of failures and victories. In fact, winners experience more failures than successes. They succeed because they pick themselves up and keep going. They don't know what it means to give up!

As we end our journey together, I want to encourage you to let God be the Lord of your life. That must be your number one priority. *Period*.

Now, repeat after me: "My current situation is not my final destination." Go ahead, say it!

Now expect change. Go for it!

Lord Jesus, I am expecting change. I will walk through change. I give up and allow You to be Lord of my everything. To You be the glory for all You have done and will do in me. Amen.

I DECLARE

I decree and declare that I am a new creature in Christ Jesus. Old things are passed away, and I now walk in newness. My future will not look like my past.

CONCLUSION

ALLOW ME TO close this work by telling you just how *awesome* God is! When you surrender your will to His, He will give you the most amazing surprises. Every day with Jesus is sweeter than the one before. Yet the choice is yours. Will you let your past dictate your future, or will you put your future in His hands?

If I had allowed statistics to project where my life would end up, I wouldn't be loving people back to life all around the world. In 2011 I stopped focusing on anything I couldn't change. I was working in retail, and instead of hating it, I decided to give it my all. I knew that if I would be faithful in little, God could trust me with much. (See Luke 16:10.) So after going through the worst of the worst times in my life, I got busy living for my future, and I quit regretting my past.

Soon, God's possibilities met my impossibility, and life became enjoyable. I developed a real passion for ministry and desired to minister full time. It took some time, but before long I was receiving invitations to preach. I traveled about twice a month, sometimes more, and was (finally!) doing what I was called to do.

On my first preaching engagement I was terrified. I remember praying and asking God to help me. I didn't know how to preach. I really didn't think I was qualified. God spoke to me and said, "You be *you*. Follow Me, and I will open the windows of heaven over you."

Spending more time with God became a priority. In His

presence I would weep and pray, sometimes for hours. My mind and my heart were changing. The anointing on my life was more real than ever before. I longed for Him and was so fulfilled in His presence. As I traveled and ministered, God showed up and wrecked the place. In my meetings I hugged people, and it was as though they began breathing again. God showed me that I was anointed to hug people back to life. It was my true calling. He would also allow me to sing prophetically to people as they experienced their healings. Although it didn't look like anything I had ever seen, I walked confidently in this anointing.

Things started happening quickly in my ministry. I began receiving invitations for radio and television interviews. I watched God restore everything in my life. While I was still working in retail, I would take my lunch break to be a guest on radio shows and do prayer calls. In my car I would pray the heavens down, then return to the cosmetics department at Bloomingdale's to finish my shift. As I began to travel more frequently, the store management always worked with my schedule. They walked with me during my time of advancement and watched God elevate me.

I began to see my social media sites explode. Twitter was my launching pad, and then I moved onto Instagram and Facebook. I used these platforms to speak of my experiences and offer solutions to people's problems. In responding to my posts, people said they felt as though I was with them in their prayer closets. People who had never heard of Jesus and never gone to church were reaching out to me for prayer.

I knew God was enlarging my territory. Nothing I said was spectacular; however, God trusted me. After traveling each weekend, I would head to work at 7:00 a.m. on Monday. During this time, God impressed me to begin a conference at my local church called Conquering Hell in High Heels. Today I stand amazed as God has blessed each endeavor. The first two years, I brought in special speakers. I knew I was not ready to minister in conferences, and yet God allowed each conference to be packed with ladies hungry for more of God. No one could stop something that God had fully endorsed.

I will always remember the first time my vehicle ran hot as I drove the interstate on the way home from work. Immediately I pulled over. Knowing I needed to allow my engine to cool down, I picked up my phone and created a video. I laughed as I began the recording with, "Hello, awesome people!"

I never dreamed that tagline would become known all over the world. My car chronicles went viral. They were shared hundreds of thousands of times. My following on social media outlets exploded some more. My whole life changed so quickly. Now I am sitting here writing the ending of my book.

God is faithful.

I still remember the day the Holy Spirit gave me permission to turn in my two-week notice. I was ecstatic! I passed the test of faithfulness. I was committed to the process, and I felt the release of something even greater about to happen. Though I was sad to close a chapter that was so dear to my heart, I knew my next chapter had begun. Bloomingdale's had been my home for five years. I went through my divorce season, my healing season, and my advancement there. Now as the door closed, I had no doubt that something even more exciting was coming.

I was ready! As I stepped out to do God's will, my calendar completely filled with engagements. I decided to begin a Tuesday morning prayer call, which was so blessed by God that people now get on thirty minutes early just to get a spot on the call.

You may ask why I am describing the blessings in my life. I want to enlarge your faith to believe that God shows no partiality. The world had given up on me, beaten me down, taken everything from me, and made me start all over again. But look at me now. Though at times it seemed as if God wasn't moving or moving quickly enough, He was moving the whole time. He proved that He's faithful. He proved to me over these last few years that if I will do my part, He will do His. He proved that He does, in fact, redeem time. He moves like the speed of lightning. He proved that when He qualifies you, it doesn't matter if you dropped out of school, have been divorced, made a million mistakes, and feel like a loser; He has the greatest comeback story in mind for you. Just forgive yourself, forgive others, and wait on God's timing.

Looking back over my life while writing this book, I can tell you this: I wouldn't trade one memory or one wrong choice that I've ever made. I wouldn't trade one tear. If I had to go back and do it all over again, I would go back and do it all the same way, except to maybe make my mistakes earlier so I could get to this place in my life sooner.

I have watched God restore my family. My sons and I can sit and talk about memories of the past, and my heart doesn't hurt anymore. They get to watch their mom love people back to life every day. They are proud of me and work in ministry with me. I have been given the greatest husband in the world, who loves me and my sons so perfectly. He is so proud of the woman I am. His love has given me permission to let my quirky style come out and play. He lets me preach in tutus and Converse sneakers. He loves the crazy, colorful stripes I put in my hair. He loves all of me, and I love all of him. I am enjoying my parents in their older years. I live right down the street from them and love doing ministry alongside them. We are all at peace.

Just eight years ago I would never have dreamed that my world would look like this. I didn't even know how to pray for all the blessings God has given me. I am thankful that I fearlessly chased after my healing and exposed my damaged heart to the greatest healer on the planet. I am thankful that I discovered the gift of goodbye in my healing process and realized that some people are only meant for lessons, not a lifetime.

As I type my last words to you, I am moved with excitement about your future. I believe in you. I believe in the God in you. Do your part and get honest with yourself. Let go of everything that's been holding you back. Don't be afraid to be vulnerable and transparent. Healing is on the other side of letting go.

SOME PEOPLE ARE ONLY MEANT FOR LESSONS, NOT A LIFETIME.
—*@RealTalkKim*

Remember that just because it's dark doesn't mean it's over. God had to turn out the lights to set up your surprise party. Everything is moving in your favor. The tide is turning, and everything that has drained you is drying up.

It's a new season!

⁓

I pray my book has blessed you more than you ever expected. I pray it has made the baby in your spiritual womb leap and you are fed in a way you have never experienced. My desire while writing the book was to connect with you in such a way that everything in your world would change. I truly believe that *we* are the ones who keep ourselves stuck in life because we aren't prepared spiritually or mentally. Storms arise, and before we know it, we are stuck like chuck. So I just know at this moment, as you are reading, that you are feeling free to live your best life. You are feeling chains being broken forever, and you are feeling hope come alive within you.

Let me remind you that if Jesus is your Lord and Savior,

you are a child of the King. He knew this day would come and you would be right here reading this book. He made this divine connection because you are so important to Him. You thought that because the curtain had closed, the production was over. However, He had to close the curtain to set up the next scene. He loves you more than you could ever know, and He never stops believing in you. I feel excitement down in my bones that you are entering the greatest season of your life. I am excited about your next season.

Let's pray:

> *Dear Lord, I believe that You are the God of the breakthrough who supplies peace, joy, strength, power, and provision for those You love. I know You love my friends, so I am asking Your blessing, in the mighty name of Jesus.*
>
> *Friend, there is power in the name of Jesus! I'm decreeing and declaring breakthrough in every area of your life. I speak healing into your body wherever there is pain. I speak healing into your family. I speak complete freedom over any addictions that have held you bound. I decree and declare complete restoration in every area of your life.*
>
> *I decree and declare that God's beautiful surprises are coming your way and the things you asked Him in prayer are coming to pass. Things you thought could never be shall be because He "is able to do exceedingly abundantly above all that we ask or think, according to the power that works in us"* (Eph. 3:20). *In Jesus' name, amen!*

ENDNOTES

CHAPTER 4: MOVE FORWARD

1. Blue Letter Bible, s.v. *"Ya`bets,"* accessed May 11, 2018, https://www.blueletterbible.org/lang/lexicon/lexicon.cfm?Strongs=H3258&t=KJV.

2. Blue Letter Bible, s.v. *"kabad,"* accessed May 11, 2018. https://www.blueletterbible.org/lang/lexicon/lexicon.cfm?Strongs=H3513&t=KJV.

3. Blue Letter Bible, *"Yisra'el,"* accessed May 11, 2018, https://www.blueletterbible.org/lang/lexicon/lexicon.cfm?Strongs=H3478&t=KJV.

CHAPTER 7: STRAIGHT OUTTA EXCUSES

1. Blue Letter Bible, *"Ben-'Owniy,"* accessed May 16, 2018, https://www.blueletterbible.org/lang/lexicon/lexicon.cfm?Strongs=H1126&t=KJV.

2. Blue Letter Bible, *"Binyamiyn,"* accessed May 16, 2018, https://www.blueletterbible.org/lang/lexicon/lexicon.cfm?Strongs=H1144&t=KJV.

CHAPTER 8: BREAKING SOUL TIES

1. "What Is the Story of Sarah and Hagar?," Got Questions, accessed May 18, 2018, https://www.gotquestions.org/Sarah-Hagar.html?.

2. "What Is the Story of Sarah and Hagar?," Got Questions.

3. "What Is the Story of Sarah and Hagar?," Got Questions.

4. "Spiritual Warfare Prayer to Break Ungodly Soul Ties," ChristiansTT.com, accessed May 18, 2018, https://

christianstt.com/spiritual-warfare-prayer-to-break-ungodly-soul-ties/.

5.   Joyce Meyer, *Battlefield of the Mind: Winning the Battle in Your Mind* (New York: Warner Books, 1995).

CHAPTER 10: FUMIGATE

1.   Google.com, s.v. "fumigate," accessed May 19, 2018.

CHAPTER 11: THE IN-BETWEEN

1.   Rick Ezell, "Sermon: While You Wait—Acts 1," Lifeway, January 1, 2014, https://www.lifeway.com/en/articles/sermon-while-you-wait-acts-1.

2.   Dr. J. Robert Clinton, director of the leadership concentration in the School of Intercultural Studies at Fuller Seminary, spent twenty-five years researching and teaching concepts he learned from studying biblical leaders. A summary of his findings can be found at Gregg Caruso, "10 Life Lessons—Parting Words From Gregg," November 30, 2014, https://sunridgechurch.org/category/supplemental-to-sermon/?.

3.   Ezell, "Sermon: While You Wait."

CHAPTER 12: WE SEE A MESS; GOD SEES A CHANCE!

1.   "The Preparation of Paul," Ligonier Ministries, accessed May, 23, 2018, https://www.ligonier.org/learn/devotionals/the-preparation-of-paul/.

2.   *English Oxford Living Dictionaries,* s.v. "disobedience," accessed May 23, 2018, https://en.oxforddictionaries.com/definition/disobedience.

3.   "What Does the Bible Say About Obedience and Disobedience?," CBN.com, accessed May 23, 2018, http://www1.cbn.com/what-does-bible-say-about-obedience-and-disobedience.

4. "What Does the Bible Say About Obedience and Disobedience?," CBN.com.

5. *English Oxford Living Dictionaries*, s.v. "self-esteem," accessed May 23, 2018, https://en.oxforddictionaries.com/definition/us/self-esteem.

CHAPTER 14: GO FOR IT!

1. Edwin Louis Cole, *Winners Are Not Those Who Never Fail but Those Who Never Quit* (Southlake, TX: Watercolor Books, 1993), 21, http://yeshuado-academy.com/resources/Never%20Quit.pdf.

2. John Mason, *An Enemy Called Average*, updated ed. (Tulsa, OK: Insight Publishing Group, 2013), 87.

3. Richard Stearns, *The Hole in Our Gospel Special Edition: What Does God Expect of Us: The Answer That Changed My Life and Might Just Change the World* (Nashville: W Publishing, 2014), 79.

4. Mason, *An Enemy Called Average*, 113.

5. Mason, *An Enemy Called Average*, 113.

6. Cole, *Winners Are Not Those Who Never Fail but Those Who Never Quit*, 121.

7. Cole, *Winners Are Not Those Who Never Fail but Those Who Never Quit*, 75.